The Alternative Bride's Guide to...

Wedding Games

Where your treasure is,
there will your heart be also.
02 08 18 29 40, 16

Ha~~~~~~~~~ ~~~~~ ~~ er
Bee,
~~~~ ~~ways with you.
Love,
Clara '13

Cover art: Cal Slayton, www.calslayton.com
Editorial services: Fraser Calhoun

ISBN 1448635071
EAN-13 9781448635078

For Gir, who made me write this before she got married, and Fraser, who is living proof that I'm "marriage material!"

Table of Contents

The Reception:

Other Events:

Bonus Section:

Introduction

As a wedding DJ, chronic bridesmaid and (yay!) a bride myself, I have been to a *lot* of weddings, and the one thing almost all brides want is a teeny tiny (okay, sometimes super gigantic) spin on the traditional wedding plan.

Gone are the days of games only for bachelorette parties and bridal showers. Today's couples often want games during some or many parts of their reception. Many also want games to keep the kids entertained, give away the centerpieces, or do away with boring old glass-clinking to make them kiss.

It's not surprising, really. Having been to more weddings than I can count, I can safely say that nothing makes a wedding more memorable than deviating – at least a little – from the norm.

The Alternative Bride's Guide to Wedding Games has 111 fabulous game ideas for every aspect of your wedding, including dozens of games for pre- and post-wedding events. You'll also love the game variations and bonus ideas that will help you to truly put your own special stamp on your wedding.

Nearly every game in this book is original - no pennies under the plates for centerpiece giveaways and no "suck 4 a buck" t-shirts at your bachelorette party. (Not that there's anything wrong with those games, but you can probably come up with those on your own!) I have included a few traditional games, as well, but only the ones that are simply too classic to be ignored... although you should still expect some fun new twists!

The games vary from simple to semi-complex, quiet sitting games to running-around-like-crazy-people games, appropriate-for-your-great-aunt-Mildred-the-nun games to hot n' spicy games... you get the idea. (See page three for more details on game ratings.)

All games are designed to bring smiles, giggles, and to help your guests get to know one another and have a great time. The result will be a relaxed atmosphere, loads of fun, and one amazing party.

...because after all, this is your special day and we want it to be memorable. I hope that these games help make your wedding as unique and entertaining as you are!

How to Use This Book

You should read through this entire book to get the most out of it, even if you're only looking for reception dinner games or bouquet tossing alternatives.

Yes, the games in this book have been organized according to wedding event type. However, most of them will work for several different types of events with little or no modification, so peruse all of the games for maximum inspiration. Even many of the kids' games would effortlessly entertain your adult guests, at least for a little while!

Feel free to modify any game according to your taste and personal style. Many games come with their own tried-and-true variation suggestions, but virtually every game in this book can be varied to accommodate the event and atmosphere that you're after.

All games are deliberately designed to appeal to a wide range of ages and personalities so that nobody feels left out or bored. A few games will exclude people with severe physical limitations, but most of the games in this book will work with just about any mix of people.

Also, most games include suggestions for prizes but, of course, giving away prizes is entirely optional. Your guests will have a blast either way!

This book comes with several helpful features to make your game planning simple and painless:

* *Photocopiable elements* for many games, including cards, puzzles, answer sheets, and more. (See the section starting on page 175.)

* *Bonus ideas* for prizes, wedding favors, keepsakes, and party themes to add a personal touch to your special day.

* *A trivia appendix* overflowing with awesome questions to be used in trivia games so you don't have to spend hours coming up with your own. (See the section starting on page 169.)

You can also visit www.theAlternativeBride.com to share your questions, game ideas, stories, and photos. I'd love to hear from you!

I want you to have as much fun as you can with this book. Hopefully your planning process will be almost as entertaining as the games themselves!

All About Ratings

Every game in this book has a special ratings box to give you an idea of what to expect of a game, as well as how (or if) it can fit into your wedding plans. Use these ratings to get quick, at-a-glance info about a game's spiciness, complexity, and activity level.

Spiciness Ratings

"Spiciness" refers to a game's degree of sexual innuendo and/or physical contact (although nothing in this book is too over the top - this is a wedding, after all!).

⊘   **Zero spice.** This rating is reserved for children's games and games that are guaranteed 100% innuendo-free.

♥   **Mild spice.** There is almost no possible way anyone could get offended by this game. Humor is cute, not sexy or dirty.

♥♥   **Medium spice.** Occasional innuendo and/or physical contact.

♥♥♥   **Pretty darn spicy.** Sexual overtones and/or plenty of physical contact. Always awesomely hilarious.

♥ to ♥♥♥   **Variable.** These ones depend on your guests. Be wary of any weirdo relatives.

up to you!   **Your call.** Customize the spiciness yourself.

Complexity Ratings

"Complexity" refers to the amount of preparation and/or materials necessary for a game, as well as how much explaining will be required for your guests to be able to play.

💣   **Piece of cake.** Little or no preparation or materials needed. Easy to explain to your guests.

💣💣   **Slightly complex.** Some preparation/materials and/or explanation required.

💣💣💣   **Fairly complex.** Moderate preparation and/or significant explanation needed. Totally worth the effort, though!

All About Ratings (cont'd.)

Activity Level Ratings

"Activity Level" refers to how much physical work is required by the participants in a given game. None of these games require Olympic-caliber endurance, but some may get the heart racing a little.

🔊 **Very calm.** Sitting only, standing more or less in one place, or very leisurely wandering around.

🔊🔊 **Some activity.** Games on your feet for more extended periods of time and/or requiring some up-and-down movement or bending.

🔊🔊🔊 **Fairly physical.** Racing games, dancing games, and games requiring upper body strength get this rating.

Remember, almost every game in this book is modifiable, so don't use the ratings as the "be all and end all" of your game selection. Be creative, have fun, and get reading!

The Alternative Bride's Guide to Wedding Games

The Reception:

Cocktail Hour Games

The cocktail reception is the official start of the party portion of your wedding day. It sets the tone for the rest of the evening, so plan a cocktail hour your guests will never forget!

The games in this section have been created specifically to help your guests mingle and break the ice. What better way to prepare for a fabulously fun wedding reception?

Since many cocktail hours are standing room only, none of these games require sitting or cumbersome props. The idea is to have simple but effective games to loosen up your crowd.

Clothes Pin Challenge

Spiciness: ♥
Complexity: 💣
Activity Level: 📣

This is a simple but super fun game for getting people moving around and mingling. Watch even the shyest of guests attack complete strangers – a perfect start to your cocktail hour!

As your guests arrive at the reception location, give each of them one clothes pin. Better yet, ask your bartenders or cocktail servers to pass out clothes pins along with the drinks. Close to the entrance or at the bar, put up a poster that explains the *Clothes Pin Challenge* rules:

* No saying the words "bride," "groom," or "wedding"
* No crossing your legs
* No dropping your cocktail napkin

Any guest who catches another guest breaking one of the rules gets to steal their clothes pin. The person with the most clothes pins at the end of the cocktail hour (or whenever you choose) gets a prize. Choose a fun, portable prize that fits with the theme and/or color scheme of the wedding.

Feel free to personalize this game by creating your own special rules that apply specifically to the newlyweds (e.g. no saying the bride's name).

My Fellow Wedding Guests

Spiciness: ♥
Complexity: 💣💣💣
Activity Level: 🔊

Here's a fabulous and entertaining way for your guests to get to know each other. In fact, they'll probably learn a thing or two about people they thought they already knew pretty well!

The object is for your guests to meet other guests with unique traits by using a series of clues on a paper. When they do identify someone, they'll write that person's name down on the paper.

For example, let's say you have one or more guests who:

* ✳ have gone to Mount Everest
* ✳ don't need glasses but wear them for the fashion statement
* ✳ used to be vegetarian
* ✳ are professional figure skaters
* ✳ were extras in a movie

You would write down these tidbits of information on a sheet of paper, leaving enough space beside each one for your contestants to write a person's name down.

The more clues you can come up with, the better (aim for at least 20). Award prizes either to the person who writes the most names down or to the one who completes all the clues first.

Bonus Idea: *Arrange the clues in a grid, like a bingo card, and have guests compete to get a line, a picture frame (all the way around the outside), the couple's initials, a blackout, etc. If you choose to play this way, you should have a few different versions so not all cards are identical.*

Ceremony Survivor

Check out the trivia appendix on page 169!

Spiciness: ❤
Complexity: 💣💣
Activity Level: 🔊

For whatever reason, trivia is the perfect go-to game to loosen up crowds of all varieties. Your cocktail reception is no exception. All you need for this game are sheets of paper for your guests, pencils (those little golf pencils work perfectly), and a list of 15 or 20 trivia questions.

Come up with questions ahead of time that apply to the ceremony your guests just attended - feel free to poach ideas from our trivia appendix (page 169). The questions should be fairly difficult so that not everyone will get them all right.

When it's time for the game, have your guests form teams of two to five people and tell them to write their answers down – not shout them out – so they don't give away any answers to their competitors. Then, start reading the questions one by one. Give teams enough time to mull the questions over and write their answers down, but don't go too slowly!

Here are a few question examples:

* What flowers are in the bride's bouquet?
* How does the groom know his best man?
* Who did a reading/sang a song?
* What music was playing as the bride came down the aisle?
* How many countries were represented by the guests at the ceremony?
* What kind of fabric is the wedding gown made of?
* What did the pew decorations look like?
* How many people were sitting in the front row?

When you've finished reading all the questions, read out the answers and let the teams score themselves. Find out the winner by asking, "Who had more than five points?" then, "Who had more than ten points?" then, "Who had 11 points?" and so on until there is only one team remaining.

Give the winning team an edible prize that they can share, such as a box of chocolates or bag of gourmet jelly beans. Have some backup prizes or tie-breaker questions ready in case two teams score the same number of points.

Guest Who!

Spiciness: ♥
Complexity: 💣💣
Activity Level: 🔊

If you're looking for an easy way to get your guests chatting with one another, look no further than *Guest Who!* This game works best if you print out the game cards on adhesive name badge paper (look online or in any big box office supply store), but you could also insert the cards into those regular plastic-holder-and-safety-pin name badges.

As your guests arrive to the cocktail reception, stick a game card to each of their backs, but make sure they don't know which one they get. The cards should have names of famous people on them, such as:

* Oprah Winfrey
* Zsa Zsa Gabor
* Tom Cruise
* Betty Boop
* Clark Gable
* Big Bird
* Britney Spears
* Sponge Bob
* Michael Jackson
* John F. Kennedy

...and so on. You'll need at least as many name badges as you have guests.

While you're handing out the badges, tell the guests that they must address people as if they were the person whose name is on their backs. They don't need to go out of their way to help anyone figure out whom they are; subtler hints are always funnier!

Give prizes to anyone who figures out their own identity or, if you'd like to keep the game going a little longer, have anyone who guesses correctly come and get another name badge. If you'd like, the person who collects the most badges by the end of the cocktail hour could win a grand prize of your choosing.

Piggyback Ride

Spiciness: ♥
Complexity: 💣
Activity Level: 🔊 🔊 🔊

When the bride and groom are arriving to their cocktail reception, announce to the guests that they're about to see a death-defying performance of strength, agility, and raw masculine power.

Then bar the couple from the room and tell them that if they want to join the party, the groom must piggyback his blushing bride before all of their guests. Tell him that once they make a complete circle of the room, they will be rewarded with cocktails and the admiration of dozens.

Encourage your guests to cheer the couple on as they race around the room. The more applause and hooting, the better the atmosphere will be set for the rest of your evening.

Make sure to have those drinks waiting for your hard-working bride and groom! You could also have a novelty trophy made that says "World's Strongest Man" or t-shirts for the couple that read: "I survived the piggyback ride!"

If the bride's dress is too restrictive for piggybacking, consider having the groom cradle her in his arms, instead. It's equally as funny and just a touch more romantic.

I Want Candy

Spiciness: ⊘
Complexity: 💣💣
Activity Level: 📢

Here's a little hot potato-esque game that's a simple way to add some fun to your cocktail hour.

Have your guests stand in a circle and give one of them a small bag of candy. Start some music – as the music plays, your guests must pass the candy around. When the music stops, the guest holding the bag of candy is eliminated (and perhaps sent to the bar as punishment!).

Here are some good song ideas for this game:

* I Want Candy
* The Candy Man
* Sugar Sugar
* Lollipop
* Can't Touch This

There are also a few variations on this game:

1) For a smaller reception size, try preparing enough bags of candy ahead of time so that the people who get eliminated can keep their candy. Have a bigger prize for the winner.

2) If you have a large number of guests coming, have several bags of candy on hand so that multiple people are eliminated every time the music stops. Let the winners keep the bags of candy.

3) Don't bother making a circle. Instead, have guests pass the bag(s) randomly about the room. Whoever's holding the candy when the music stops wins!

Cocktail Contest

Spiciness: ♥♥
Complexity: 💣💣💣
Activity Level: 🔊

This game is perfect for smaller wedding receptions or receptions at home. You'll want to chat with the bar staff ahead of time to make sure this game is okay with them. It will be cheaper if you're allowed to bring in your own liquor and mixers.

Other than booze and mixers, you'll need some olives, berries, cherries, orange slices, cinnamon sticks, those little umbrellas, and Dixie cups for this game. The object is to pit your guests against one another to see who can make the most delicious cocktail.

Choose three or four guests to compete (or use members of the wedding party if they're back from the photo session). They can use whatever alcohol, mixers, and garnishes are available to them. Announce a time limit – three minutes is usually sufficient – and then set them to work.

During this time, add some extra amusement by providing some running commentary ("Olives and peppermint schnapps? I'm skeptical!") and playing some suspenseful music, like the *Mission Impossible* or "Jeopardy" theme songs.

When they are finished, have the contestants display their work proudly. The judges (i.e. your remaining guests) should be asked to take esthetics into consideration when making their final decision.

Next, pour small samples of each drink into Dixie cups and pass them around. It doesn't matter if all the guests don't get to try each drink. Just pass them around to as many people as possible. It will be helpful if you have different colors of Dixie cups so guests can tell which drink belongs to which contestant.

When the drinks have been sampled, it's time to vote. Guests can cast their ballot for their favorite drink through rambunctious applause. The loudest applause will tell you who should get the prize for the best cocktail!

Alternatively, if the bride and groom are attending their cocktail reception, make them the judges. This is an easier option because only the happy couple must sample the drinks, not all the guests.

You don't need to use alcohol to play this game. If you're hosting an alcohol-free party, guests can compete to make the best virgin cocktails, smoothies, or sundaes.

Bonus Idea: If the best drink was especially wonderful, have the bartender put it on the menu as your signature cocktail for the reception. Name the cocktail in honor of the winner (as in "The Betty" or "The Mike")!

The Fashionista Awards

Spiciness: ⊘
Complexity: 💣✴
Activity Level: 📢

Here's a quick and easy game to set a light-hearted tone for both the cocktail reception and the rest of the evening.

Before the big day, dream up a few "fashion categories" that guests could win without even knowing they were in a contest. Possible categories include:

* Best Dressed Lady
* Best Dressed Gentleman
* Closest Match to the Wedding Colors
* Most Tropical Outfit (works anywhere; not just for destination weddings)
* Goofiest Getup (only include this one if you know someone who can take a joke, such as the groom's brother who rented a powder blue tuxedo especially for the occasion)

When the end of the cocktail hour is approaching, have your MC make an announcement that there are a lot of beautiful people at this wedding and it's time to honor the best of the best.

Have funny prizes ready, such as a tiara and wand for the "Best Dressed Gentleman" winner, a plastic lei and oversized novelty sunglasses for the "Most Tropical Outfit" winner, a star-shaped badge (like a sheriff's badge) for the "Goofiest Getup" winner, etc. Make sure the prize is something wearable so they can proudly display their awards all evening!

Secret Snacks

Spiciness: ⊘
Complexity: 💣💣
Activity Level: 📢

This is an amusing little game to keep your guests' appetites down while they're waiting for dinner. You'll need small numbered dishes (paper bowls work well), several different kinds of cocktail-type snacks, and sheets of paper with as many numbers as you have snacks.

On each cocktail table, place a variety of snacks, such as:

* honey-roasted peanuts
* wasabi peas
* yogurt-covered pretzels
* chocolate-covered raisins
* flavored potato chips
* walnuts (de-shelled)
* hazelnut chocolates
* Peanut Butter M&Ms

Number the dishes that the snacks are in so that "number one" dishes all contain wasabi peas, "number two" dishes are all beer nuts, and so on. Keep a master list so you can tabulate scores at the end.

Tell guests that they will play in teams to sample the snacks and identify what they've eaten. They should write the snack names down beside the numbers on their sheet of paper. Whoever correctly identifies the most snacks after a set period of time is the winner!

To increase the mingling, don't put every type of snack on every table. Instead, put only two or three different kinds on each table. That way, teams will have to move about the room to locate all the snacks.

To make this game easier to plan (and a bit more sophisticated), use different flavors of gourmet jelly beans instead of snacks - there are literally dozens of different flavors available, from café latte to cotton candy to jalapeño and beyond (just do a search on the Internet). Separate the different flavors and play as described above.

Picture Perfect Puzzles

Spiciness: ♥
Complexity: 💣💣💣
Activity Level: 🔊

Before the wedding day, dig up some fun photos of the bride and groom. You could use old vacation photos, Halloween photos, ones from when they were little kids, etc. The photos must be digital, so be sure to scan any that you only have prints for.

Transform the photos into puzzles by taking them to a developer who offers this service. Usually any big box store that offers photo finishing has this feature, so you shouldn't have a problem getting this done inexpensively.

If you're computer-savvy, you can also do this at home. Just visit an office supply store to pick up printable puzzle paper.

Bring the puzzles to your cocktail reception and put one on each cocktail table, making sure the pieces are scattered a bit. You'll want the puzzles to be small enough that people can easily put the puzzle together and fit a few drinks on the table at the same time. Award the puzzles as prizes to whoever completes them.

For a more challenging variation, just make one big puzzle and scatter the pieces on the various tables. Your guests must work together to solve the puzzle! Have an extra table handy so that your guests have somewhere to work on the puzzle together.

The Reception:

Dinner Games

Dinner games can be tricky because your guests are already doing something: eating.

However, even dinners have their fair share of downtime. No guest enjoys waiting their turn for the buffet! The right games can fill the time without disrupting the main event.

Games are also perfect for those tables full of "miscellaneous" guests who don't know each other at all. Eliminate awkwardness using games designed to get your guests laughing and interacting.

This section also contains "bridal party only" games, which will put on a pretty hilarious show for your guests without them leaving their seats for a second.

Choose one or a few of these games to make your wedding dinner entertaining and memorable.

Wedding Scramble

Make photocopies of page 177!
(instructions on page 176)

Spiciness: ⊘
Complexity: 💣
Activity Level: 📢

This is a deceptively simple pencil-and-paper game that will do a good job of getting your guests chatting while they're waiting for their turn to raid the buffet. It's also handy for keeping kids busy so the grown-ups can linger a little over their coffee.

All you have to do is come up with 15 or 20 wedding-related words and then mix up the letters of each word. For example, the phrase "wedding ring" can become "wingedd grin." (It could also be "dgniwde rgni" if you're too busy arguing with the caterer to discover semi-real words.)

Write the scrambled words on a sheet of paper, one per line (or use the reproducible on page 177 in this book - answers are on page 176). Make sure there is space beside each word for your guests to write the answers.

This game is a great time-occupier or, if you'd like to give away prizes, you could make up some little goodie bags for any guest that finishes the puzzle. (Note: this is not a good centerpiece giveaway game because more than one person per table may complete the scramble.)

Bonus Idea: Customize your Wedding Scramble *pages by including a photo of the happy couple and/or printing them on stationery that matches your color scheme.*

Bonus Idea: Get some personalized pencils for each table setting - they can double as your wedding favors!

Marriage for Dummies

Make photocopies of page 178!

Spiciness: ♥ to ♥♥♥
Complexity: 💣
Activity Level: 📢

This game will range from sweet to totally off color, just like your guests (oh, Uncle Ernie...). It works best with small to mid-sized receptions, but if you're willing to sort through all the entries it will work just as well at large ones.

At each place setting, put a small card (recipe cards work great) with the words "My best marriage advice is..." written at the top and "From:" at the bottom (you can use ours on page 178). Throughout dinner, guests can jot down their best marriage advice to the newly-weds.

You can ask your guests to bring the cards up to the master of ceremonies when they're filled in or, better yet, get your servers to pick them up. It's a good idea to pre-prepare a small, decorated box or basket as a card collector.

Throughout the dinner (and especially in between courses or during other lulls) have your MC read out some of the best marriage advice cards. "Best" can mean a lot of things: funny, touching, spicy... you get the idea. You'll be surprised at how creative your guests will be with this game!

Marriage for Dummies is a great prize-awarding game, too. Create categories for the best advice, including:

* The Most Practical
* The Funniest
* The Best Bedroom Advice
* The Silliest
* The Best Overall

...and whatever else you come up with. Give awards to the winners of each category. Consider having some novelty trophies or medals made, or simply buy some chocolates, small trinkets, or the like.

Bonus Idea: *Make a collage of your marriage advice cards and frame it for a charming memento of your wedding reception.*

The Mister or the Missus?

Check out the trivia appendix on page 169!

Spiciness: ♥ ♥
Complexity: 💣 💣
Activity Level: 🔊

This is another great game to fill the time your guests would otherwise spend waiting impatiently for their next course. It's a bit more complex because you've got to prepare a trivia list and a few signs ahead of time, but it's nothing that can't be accomplished in a martini-filled afternoon with the bridesmaids.

Divide the bridal party up into two teams: men versus women. You may also want to include the parents of the bride and groom for extra fun. Give each team two signs, one that says "Mister" and one that says "Missus." The signs must be big enough for the guests to read from a distance.

Next, have the game host ask a series of questions, such as:

 ✳ Who steals the blankets?
 ✳ Who's going to do the most diaper changing?
 ✳ Who would win a snoring competition?
 ✳ Who will go gray first?
 ✳ Who's the better dancer?

After each question, have the teams hold up either the "Mister" or "Missus" sign. You're guaranteed to get tons of laughter and goofy commentary from the teams, the guests and, of course, your victims: the bride and groom.

This is a perfect during-dinner game because everyone stays in their seats and there is virtually no setup involved. Make it even easier by using the trivia appendix at the back of this book for inspiration!

Bonus Idea: Instead of the words "Mister" or "Missus," use the bride and groom's names or, better yet, use big pictures of each of them in less-than-photogenic moments.

Bonus Idea: Instead of having signs and different teams, make it bride versus groom. Seat them back-to-back and have each of them remove their shoes and swap one shoe with their spouse. When the game host asks a question, they should each hold up the shoe corresponding to the answer. People will get lots of laughs with this one!

Roman Hands

Spiciness: up to ♥♥♥
Complexity: 💣
Activity Level: 📢

This is a great little game to attempt mid- to late-dinner when everyone's got a little bit of liquor in them. I promise you'll get a lot of laughter and hopefully a little blushing on the part of the happy couple.

At some point, have the bride and groom stand up in front of their guests and announce that if they want their dessert/coffee/after-dinner drink/bathroom break, they'll have to pass the time-honored challenge of *Roman Hands*.

All you need for this game are a blindfold and three clothes pins or big paperclips.

Blindfold the bride and place the clothes pins in three clever places on the groom's body. Tell the bride (and the guests) that she must locate the clothes pins before she will be released. Your guests will love watching the bride grope for her freedom.

If the bride is really struggling, have guests shout, "Hotter!" or "Colder!" as she attempts to locate the clothes pins. It's a simple way to increase the interaction and energy level in the room.

Put the clothes pins in interesting places like on the groom's sock, in his hair, on his cummerbund, on the seat of his pants... you get the idea. Feel free to be as risqué with the clothes pin placement as the newlyweds will be comfortable with, and don't be surprised if the bride takes it to the next level!

Russian Fingers

Spiciness: ♥♥♥
Complexity: 💣
Activity Level: 📢

If you didn't feel that *Roman Hands* was quite enough to embarrass your bride and groom, ramp it up with *Russian Fingers*!

No blindfolds this time – just a single hard-boiled egg. (Insert ominous music here.)

That's right, this time the poor bride has to insert the egg into the bottom of one of her groom's pant legs and move it up one leg and down the other side. If the bride is of the spunky variety, make sure to tell her that the groom's pants must remain on for the entire game!

To vary this game (and/or spread the pressure out a bit), have extra eggs for couples who think they can beat the bride and groom's time. Alternatively, make the whole bridal party do it, as long as they're couples, or get the parents of the newlyweds up there (if you're brave enough to ask!).

If you do add more couples into the mix, consider having small prizes for the winners. You could also award the "used" eggs to the fastest couple as a semi-disgusting gag award. Eww...

Another variation possibility is to use two eggs at the same time. Each egg must simultaneously travel up one pant leg and down the other. Try scaring the groom a little by telling him that only one of the eggs is hard-boiled!

Who Wants to be a Five-dollar-aire?

Check out the trivia appendix on page 169!

Spiciness: ♥♥
Complexity: 💣💣
Activity Level: 📢

This trivia game really brings out the competitive side of your guests. Everyone gets a chance to compete for the title of "Most Couple-Savvy." This game is extra fun if you can dig up some suspenseful game show-type music to go along with the question reading. (Try asking your DJ.)

To prepare, you'll need a fairly long list of trivia questions of progressive difficulty. Make sure all of the questions have at least something to do with the bride and/or groom.

Have all your guests stand up for the challenge. Those who answer the first question correctly can remain standing. Those who get it wrong (or just don't know) have to sit down - they're out.

Here are a few examples to give you an idea of how the questions should be ordered in terms of difficulty:

* Where did the bride and groom meet?
* Did they live together before they got engaged/married?
* Where are they going on their honeymoon?
* What color car does the couple have?
* Where did they go to school?
* What is the bride's middle name?
* What is the groom's favorite sports team?
* What does the bride like better: chocolate cake or carrot cake?

It's a good idea to include some true or false questions, yes/no questions, or other either/or questions so that even guests who don't know the couple that well will be able to play for at least a little while. Also, the hilarity factor gets raised a bit if you ask questions that the bride and groom themselves may not know the answer to, such as "What time of day was the groom born?" (And make them sit down when they get it wrong!)

At any rate, the questions will have to get more difficult as the crowd standing gets sparser.

As the title suggests, award a five-dollar bill to the winner or, if you prefer, have several five-dollar bills on hand in case there is a tie between a few especially clever guests. Alternatively, be true to the game's namesake and make a big million dollar novelty check as a gag prize for the winner.

Accolades for the Experts

Spiciness: ♥
Complexity: 💣💣
Activity Level: 🔊

This is a charming little game that is a great way to kick off the speeches or fill a lull during the guests' table time. All of the preparation is done beforehand so it's guaranteed to go flawlessly on the big day.

If the bride and groom are up for it, they are the perfect people to host this game, but the MC will do nicely as well.

Make a little joke about how planning a wedding is proof that marriage has its ups and downs, and then talk about how if the couple is really looking for a lifetime of happiness, all the expert advice they could ever need is right here in the room tonight.

Give awards to the couples at the reception who reflect some of the qualities of a super-successful marriage. Remember to think of the categories, choose the winners, and pick up the awards ahead of time!

Some category ideas are:

* The Longest Marriage
* The Most Adventurous Couple
* The Best Comedy Duo
* The Craziest Couple (because every good marriage needs a little dose of insanity!)
* The Coolest Honeymoon
* The Best Parents (this should probably be split between the parents of the bride and groom unless you want to create some drama!)

You can treat the whole game like an Academy Awards ceremony, complete with sealed envelopes, a red carpet, and Oscar-shaped trophies, or give away nice prizes like restaurant vouchers, gift baskets, or V.I.P. invites to the bride and groom's home for an evening of champagne and dessert.

Either way, this is a heartwarming game that is a wonderful way for the happy couple to tip their hats to the people who've really inspired them along the way.

Celebrity Match

Spiciness: ♥
Complexity: 💣💣
Activity Level: 📢

This game is an easy way to get your guests chatting to one another around their dinner tables because it involves teamwork and everyone's favorite topic: celebrity gossip. That makes it the perfect icebreaker, even for your shyest guests.

To prepare for this game, you'll need to make a couple of dozen different game cards, each with a celebrity's name on it. Remember to make enough sets of game cards for each table at your reception. The celebrities you choose should be fairly well-known and, most importantly, they have to have been married to another celebrity at some point in their careers. (To find inspiration for your cards, just do an Internet search for "Celebrity couples.")

Put the cards in nice boxes or baskets on each dinner table. You could also include a small paper that explains the purpose of the cards, or just have your MC explain before dinner gets rolling.

To play *Celebrity Match*, one guest pulls a card and reads it out loud to their table. As a group, the table should try to figure out to whom the celebrity on the card is/was married. If they can think of more than one spouse for a given celebrity, all the better!

Have each table tally their points - it's one point for each correct spouse named. The table with the most points wins! You can award prizes, if you'd like, or just congratulate everyone on their celeb gossip prowess.

Bonus Idea: *Play this game at any function with a sit-down meal, such as your rehearsal dinner. It's such a simple way to add an element of fun whenever there's even the tiniest lull at the table.*

Pop the Question

Check out the trivia appendix on page 169!

Spiciness: ♥ ♥
Complexity: 💣 💣
Activity Level: 📢 📢

This game gives the phrase "pop the question" a whole new meaning. You'll need some balloons, trivia questions, some goofy prizes, and some even goofier prizes. This is a good game for right after dinner, before the dance gets rolling.

To prepare, print out and roll up some pieces of paper with the trivia questions on them and insert them into the balloons right before you blow them up.

Select some pairs of people to participate in this game – make sure you have at least one balloon per group of two people. They can be couples, like the bride and groom, their parents, or other engaged couples, or you could choose pairs of brothers, sisters, bridesmaids, groomsmen... your imagination is the limit!

Give each team a blown-up balloon and tell them that inside is a trivia question about the bride and groom that, if answered correctly, will earn them a prize. Then tell them that they must pop the balloon as a team using any means necessary except their hands or feet.

Your guests will love watching the teams wriggle around trying to pop their balloons. Make sure to tell those bystanders to cheer their favorite teams on!

Once a team pops a balloon, have them read out their trivia question. It's a good idea to make these questions true or false, so they have a reasonable chance of winning a prize. If they answer correctly, award them a prize. If not, have some gag gifts standing by, such as bananas, a tape of a bad '80s band from a second-hand store, some crazy boxer shorts (not from a second-hand store!)... you get the idea. Either that, or just return them to their seats empty-handed.

If you'd like to keep this game going, have extra balloons on hand and let teams take a new balloon after they've correctly answered the trivia question inside the previous balloon. You can either award them a prize for every correct question or just give the team who answered the most questions a big prize at the end.

For a simpler version of this game, eliminate the trivia portion altogether. Just blow up some balloons and have teams pop them (remember, no hands or feet!). The team with the most popped balloons wins!

Missing Mate

Spiciness: up to you!
Complexity: 💣
Activity Level: 📢 📢

The only things you need for this guaranteed-to-be-awesome game are a blindfold and as many willing participants as desired. Plan for this game to occur right at the end of dinner before the dance gets rolling, or sometime around the cake cutting, when lots of people will be milling around anyway.

This game usually runs best if the groom (the blindfold-ee) has an escort, so as not to injure himself or any innocent bystanders.

Once the groom is blindfolded, line up all the people who will be participating side by side. Remember to include the bride somewhere in the mix! Then, it's the groom's job to feel each person and determine whether or not that person is his new wife.

Remember, this game is not for women only – it always gets extra laughs if you throw men and children into the mix. Don't be surprised when the groom doesn't manage to rule out his best man immediately!

There are tons of variations for this game to increase or decrease the spiciness rating:

Tamer versions:

  * No touching. Instead, each person says, "Hello, honey!" in their best imitation of the bride's voice. (Giggles guaranteed.)
  * Handshakes only.
  * Play some music and have the groom take turns dancing with each guest.

Dinner Games

* No lineup - play a "Marco Polo" version where the groom shouts out his wife's name and she responds from somewhere in the sea of people. For example, he calls out, "Lauri!" and then tries to walk in the direction of his wife calling, "Barry!" The other guests can do their best to hide the bride and/or impede the groom.

Spicier versions (no kids allowed!):

* Make the groom feel each person's legs (extra laughs with the male guests!)
* Have the groom kiss each person on the cheek and have the guest kiss him back – can the groom identify his wife based on cheeks alone?
* Tushy grabbing – can the groom identify his wife based on "cheeks" alone?
* No lineup – the bride hides in the crowd and everyone can only say one phrase: "Ooooh, baby!" Let the groom find his lady's voice amidst the sea of phonies!

Merry Cherries

Spiciness: ♥ ♥
Complexity: 💣
Activity Level: 📢 📢

Introducing yet another fabulous way to torment the bride and groom a little before sending them off into marital bliss:

(Hey, why should they have all the fun?)

All you need for this game is a fairly long piece of string (four or five feet), a cherry, a chair, and a helper.

Tie the string to the cherry and have the helper stand on the chair and dangle it before the bride and groom. Tell the bride and groom that they've got to work together to eat the cherry. No hands allowed!

Sounds simple enough, but the newlyweds will really need to dust off their teamwork skills to accomplish this task, especially when the "helper" starts bobbing the cherry up and down!

To keep the fun going, have extra cherries and strings on hand for whoever would like to challenge the bride and groom's record. Give the couple with the fastest time a prize.

Wedding Day Showdown

Spiciness: ♥
Complexity: 💣 💣
Activity Level: 📣 📣 📣

Here's a game to put the wedding party on the spot. You can make this game as simple or as elaborate as you'd like, so the props you'll need will vary. This one works best with an even number of brides-maids and groomsmen, and don't forget the referee!

Announce that it's time for the *Wedding Day Showdown*, during which Team Bride and Team Groom will be competing for the gold medal!

This game is essentially a relay race with a few challenges designed especially to get your guests laughing. Potential relay events include:

* Run to the gift table to retrieve a wedding present
* Serve cupcakes to one person at three different tables - and no table can have more than one cupcake at a time!
* The classic egg-on-a-spoon relay (hard-boiled, please!)
* Retrieve one of each type of coin (penny, nickel, dime, and quarter) from wedding guests
* Piggyback one teammate around the dance floor
* A three-legged race
* Every team member eats one package of saltines (I mean the two-cracker kind, not a whole box!)
* Pass a balloon between teammates using only your necks
* Come up with a wedding cheer (save this one for last)

You can use only one activity that each person on the team must per-form, or combine several to make it a triathlon (or some other "-ath-lon"). You may want to use a chair as a marker for activities such as the egg-on-a-spoon race to set a clear point for the team to reach be-fore turning around to come back to the start line. Throughout the game, the referee should be encouraging the crowd to cheer the teams on!

It's smart to include at least a few activities that don't involve sprinting because otherwise your high-heeled ladies will be at a distinct disadvantage. Also, don't choose anything that's too messy so no one ruins their clothing.

To turn up the cuteness factor, include your flower girl and ring bearer in the fun, and don't forget the medals for the winning team!

Bingo Bliss

Make photocopies of pages 180-181!
(instructions on page 179)

Spiciness: ♥
Complexity: 💣 💣
Activity Level: 🔊 🔊 🔊

A marital twist on grandma's favorite game, *Bingo Bliss* is sure to be a crowd pleaser. You'll need enough 5x5 playing cards for your guests as well as game cards for the game host. Make your own or steal the templates on pages 180-181!

Instead of numbers in the squares, your bingo cards should have pictures of wedding-related items, such as bells, a cake, a bouquet, a garter belt, a wedding gift... you get the idea. For every picture that you have, you'll need an identical one on a game card.

Remember, all the cards should be different - this is bingo! Get the girls together and spend an afternoon with a photocopier and some margaritas, or make it easier by giving your guests blank cards at the reception and asking them to think of their own wedding-related items and draw them in the empty squares on their cards.

The host draws a game card and calls out the picture. Guests mark off any pictures they have on their card. You could put some bingo dabbers, pencils, or jelly beans on the tables to use as markers.

Continue drawing cards until a guest shouts out "Bingo!" Before the game, you'll have to decide what "bingo" actually is. It could be a line, a heart shape, the initial of the bride and groom... it's up to you!

Award a prize (bingo dabbers, anyone?) to the winner and have backup prizes on hand in case there are multiple winners.

Personalize this game by including pictures of the bride and groom on the game cards. Just cut out little pictures of their heads, photocopy them onto the cards, and presto! Instant, personalized goofiness!

The Reception:

Make-You-Kiss Games

It's very common for newlyweds to want to include games to make them kiss, in honor of the classic wedding tradition.

It's also common for couples to want to do away with boring old glass-clinking in favor of something a bit more original.

This section is devoted to alternative ideas to coerce a little lip-locking. The ideas range from sweet to wacky and every single one is guaranteed to bring some smiles while the happy couple puts on a little show for the guests.

Sorry, glass-clinking, but let's face it: your day is well past done.

Hips for Lips

Spiciness: ♥ ♥
Complexity: 💣
Activity Level: 🔊 🔊 🔊

The bride and groom have planned this big party for everyone – why should they do all the work now? All this game takes is a hula-hoop, either one per table or set up a few in front of the head table for all to see.

Have your MC announce that there will be no glass-clinking tonight. Instead, any guest who wants to see the happy couple lock lips must first perform a semi-impressive feat of hula-hooping.

For an additional laugh factor, include this caveat: the couple will only kiss for as long as the hula-hooper is able to keep the hula-hoop off the ground. This way, most of your kisses will only last for a peck or two... but be prepared for your eight-year old flower girl who's been brushing up on her hula-hoop skills all summer!

Bonus Idea: If you're having a beach wedding, an outdoor barbecue reception, or a beach party/Hawaiian theme, have leis made for all your guests and give them away as wedding favors!

Singing for Smooches

Spiciness: ♥
Complexity: 💣
Activity Level: 🔊

This is a great game to loosen up your guests and make them work for those kisses!

The concept is simple: in order for the couple to kiss, a table must stand up and sing a song together. Before the party, either come up with a list of songs your guests can choose from or pick a theme and make the guests think up their own.

For example, let's say your theme is tropical songs (perfect for a destination wedding!). Your guests might think of the following:

* (You put the lime in the) Coconut
* Hot, Hot, Hot
* Surfin' Safari

... and only heaven knows what else!

Here's a list of song theme ideas to get your creative juices flowing:

* Early '90s dance songs (à la "Whoomp! There it is!")
* Songs in which guests replace names with the names of the couple. Everyone will laugh when "Roxanne" is changed to "Katie" or "Bingo" is changed to "Chris" (as in "There was a farmer had a dog and Chris was his name-o, C-H-R-I-S...")
* Children's songs
* Songs with a reference to a color
* Super-duper sappy songs

Choose a theme that best ties in with the overall theme of the wedding or just the personal tastes of the newlyweds.

Luck of the Dice

Spiciness: ♥
Complexity: 💣
Activity Level: 📢

This is a piece-of-cake game to prepare for because all you need is a pair of dice for each table.

The rules are simple: guests must pair off at each table. At any point during the dinner, the pair may roll the dice. If they roll an even number, the bride and groom must kiss. If they roll an odd number, the pair of guests must kiss!

This game will definitely garner some chuckles, especially if your Uncle Larry and Uncle Wayne pair off together. Be prepared for those with a penchant for gambling to challenge the newlyweds on more than one occasion, especially if they're on a losing streak!

Increase the spiciness of this game by making specific dice combinations equal specific romantic maneuvers. For example, two ones (that's "snake eyes" for all you Vegas newbies) could mean the kiss must include a romantic dip. Two sixes could mean that the bride and groom must each kiss someone in their wedding party.

Bonus Idea: *If you're getting married in Vegas and having the party at home, give your whole reception a Vegas feel with big dice and poker chip centerpieces, neon lights, and playing cards for place cards.*

Shake Your Groove Thing

Spiciness: ♥
Complexity: 💣💣
Activity Level: 📣📣📣

Nothing beats watching a bunch of uncoordinated people wiggle and wobble about to induce some public displays of affection, especially once the wine has gone around a time or two.

For this game, tell your guests that if they want to see you kiss, they can forget the clinking and start moving! In order for the newlyweds to kiss, guests must dance for the couple's viewing pleasure.

Prepare a CD of funny dance songs ahead of time. Some possible songs to include are:

* Stayin' Alive
* The Chicken Dance
* You Sexy Thing
* Chariots of Fire
* Cotton Eye Joe
* Thriller
* Dancing Queen
* Girls Just Wanna Have Fun

* Vogue
* Tango music (something about it turns people into goofballs)
* The Hamster Dance
* We Are Family
* Play That Funky Music
* The Hokey Pokey

Don't worry about including the whole song and certainly don't make your guests dance for that long. Just put them on the spot for about ten seconds or so. A good DJ will also be able to gauge how long it should last (i.e. particularly hilarious guests deserve a few extra seconds to strut their stuff!).

Bonus Idea: If you're having a theme wedding of any kind, match the songs to your theme. Destination weddings can have reggae or beach music, for example.

48

Lip-Lock Trivia

Check out the trivia appendix on page 169!

Spiciness: ♥
Complexity: 💣💣
Activity Level: 🔊

Trivia is a good game for almost any occasion, and this is especially true for a wedding. It's a fabulous way to liven up a tradition that can be a little – let's be honest – tired.

Prepare some trivia questions ahead of time. You'll need at least a few for every table and the more the better. These can be questions about the couple and their wedding, weddings in general, romantic movie trivia... just pick a theme and go with it!

Divide the trivia cards between the tables. When the guests have sat down to dinner, tell them that if they want to see the newlyweds lock lips, they'll have to answer a question correctly. To get the room's attention, the person should stand up and shout, "Trivia!" If a guest fails to answer correctly, the bride and groom don't have to kiss.

You could also raise the bar by punishing your guests for their lack of nuptial knowledge. For example, the offending guest could have to kiss someone, wear a silly hat (to be passed on the next time someone gets a question wrong), or eat a bowl of Jell-o with no utensils.

You could also have the questions asked by table, which would reduce the number of times the bride and groom would have to stand up and kiss. If the table gets a question wrong, you could make them sing a song, perform the Chicken Dance, or all kiss each other.

Here are a few trivia ideas for inspiration:

  * How many guests are at the wedding?
  * How old were the bride and groom when they met?

✳ Who told Scarlett she should be kissed "often, and by someone who knows how?"
✳ Who is taller, the bride or the groom?
✳ Name three Beatles songs containing the word "love."
✳ Where did the groom propose?

Don't forget to check out our trivia appendix on page 169 for tons more ideas!

Bonus Idea: Use decorative metal or wooden "trees" as centerpieces and hang the trivia questions from them, along with flowers or small ornaments that match your color scheme.

Monkey See, Monkey Do

Spiciness: ♥ to ♥♥♥
Complexity: 💣
Activity Level: 📢

A wise person once said, "Imitation is the sincerest form of flattery." Why not flatter your guests on your big day by putting them in the hot seat for a moment or two?

In this super simple game, if anyone wants you to kiss, they first must perform the kiss they'd like to see themselves. There are no props for this game, only a brave bride and groom who are willing to go as far as their guests will!

For a variation on this game, leave the glass-clinking in, but whoever initiated it will have to imitate the kiss that the bride and groom perform. This is a perfect twist for a daring couple that isn't afraid to make their guests squirm a little.

Either way, make sure your photographer is handy!

Bonus Idea: Give away those gummy red lips candies as wedding favors to commemorate all the crazy kissing!

Love Limericks

Make photocopies of page 182!

Spiciness: ❤ to ❤❤❤
Complexity: 💣💣
Activity Level: 🔊

This game brings out the poet in your guests and is a fantastic way to encourage your guests to interact with one another. All you need are pencils and paper for each table, as well as guests who are willing to resurrect their inner leprechauns.

In order for the bride and groom to kiss, guests must create a limerick that is somehow related to the happy couple. When it's ready, they can stand up at their table and shout, "Limerick!"

For those of you who didn't do so well in your Irish poetry classes, a limerick is a five-line poem whose first, second, and fifth lines rhyme with each other. The third and fourth lines also rhyme with each other, and they are shorter than the others. (There are rules about syllables, too, but let's not get carried away!)

Here is a super awesome example, painstakingly composed by yours truly:

There once were two kids, Rob and Carrie,
Who were very excited to marry.
They both like to dance
And wear polka-dot pants
And hang out with their friends Trish and Gerry.

Thank you, thank you!

Anyway, once the guests in question have stood up and recited their limerick, the bride and groom must kiss. For extra fun, you could also give out prizes for the bride and groom's favorite little ditties!

Don't forget to check out our photocopiable *Love Limericks* sheet on page 182. Customize it by including a photo of the newlyweds. Just paste the happy couple over one of the shamrocks before you make your photocopies!

Bonus Idea*: Have guests come up to the podium to recite their limericks and then give them to the MC, who can collect them as an entertaining addition to the couple's wedding scrapbook.*

Bonus Idea*: Pre-print the limerick sheets to match your wedding colors and decorate the tables with four-leaf clover pencils and erasers, as well as green-themed centerpieces.*

Pucker Up Putting Game

Spiciness: ♥
Complexity: 💣✳
Activity Level: 🔊 🔊

Calling all golf fans: here's a great opportunity for your guests to show off their putting skills (or lack thereof)!

For this game, you'll need a putter or two as well as some kind of hole. If you want to get fancy, you can rent or buy a practice putting green, but really all you need is some kind of can or cup that you can place on its side.

You've probably guessed by now that anyone who gets a hole-in-one earns the right to watch the bride and groom kiss. However, you can make this game a little more interesting by also having prizes on hand for the best "stunt putts." Think putts behind the back, through the legs, using the club upside down or as a pool cue... you get the drift.

You could also have one of those super-cool shiny tournament jackets to give to the person who sinks the first putt or makes the most holes-in-one throughout the course of the evening.

Bonus Idea: *If you've got a sports-crazy couple, add other sports-themed challenges. For example, you could have a basketball competition - people would have to throw a basketball into a net (perfect if your hall already has a net mounted on the wall) from behind a set point. If they make the shot, the couple locks lips; if not, 50 pushups! (Oh, you're just joking... right?)*

The Language of Love

Spiciness: ♥
Complexity: 💣
Activity Level: 🔊

The Language of Love is a cute, simple game that tests your guests' foreign vocabulary knowledge. No preparation is required, so this one really couldn't be easier to play!

In order to make the couple kiss, a table must say the word "love" in a foreign language. First, they'll need to get the room's attention; for example, they could all stand up together and then the MC would announce that that table is ready to make the bride and groom do some smooching. Of course, good old-fashioned glass-clinking will do the trick, too.

For your reference, here is "love" in a few different languages (in case you suspect your guests might be making them up!):

* French: *amour*
* Italian: *amore*
* Spanish: *amor*
* German: *liebe*
* Danish: *kærlighed*
* Indonesian: *cinta*
* Filipino: *pagmamahal*
* Greek: *eros* or *agape*
* Albanian: *dashuria*
* Hebrew: אהבה (pronounced "ahava")
* Korean: 사랑 (pronounced "*sarahng*")
* Latin: *amare*

You'll probably be surprised by how much knowledge your guests have tucked away in their brains, but even if they aren't language masters, you'll still have some fun as they get more and more creative with their answers. I mean, Pig Latin and Klingon *do* count as languages, don't they?

Whose Line?

Spiciness: ♥
Complexity: 💣💣
Activity Level: 🔊

This is the perfect make-you-kiss game for a couple that loves movies or is having a flashy red carpet wedding reception.

Place sealed envelopes at each table (just like at the Oscars!). Each envelope should contain a small piece of paper that has three or four movie quotes, such as:

* Stellllllllllllllaaaaaaaaa!!!
* There's no place like home.
* I'm going to make him an offer he can't refuse.
* I think this is the beginning of a beautiful friendship.
* I'm the king of the world!

If you're stuck for ideas, just do an Internet search for "movie quotes." There are entire websites dedicated to the topic. (Those people must have a lot of free time.)

When a guest wants to make the newlyweds kiss, they must open the envelope and identify the movie that one of the quotes is from. If they guess the movie correctly, the bride and groom kiss. If you'd like, you could have them move on to the next quote to see if they can make the couple kiss again. Alternatively, you could award a prize to guests who can also name the actors or the year the movie came out.

For a variation on this game, put the paper containing the quotes inside balloons at the tables. Fill the balloons with helium so they will make nice centerpieces. When someone wants to make the couple kiss, they should pop a balloon to access their movie quote. This is a dramatic (and loud!) way to let the whole room know that there's about to be some smooching going on.

The Reception:

Centerpiece Giveaway Games

Let's be honest: no matter how beautiful your centerpieces are, what are you going to do with 12 of them once the wedding is over?

Centerpiece giveaway games evolved out of sheer necessity, but unfortunately their evolution didn't get much past a sticker under the lucky chairs or the infamous "pass the buck" game. (Ho-hum.)

That's why I've included ten original games to make the centerpiece giveaway portion of your evening a lively and entertaining event.

... because if you've got to part with your gorgeous centerpieces, at least do it in style!

Your Most Famous Guests

Spiciness: ♥
Complexity: 💣
Activity Level: 📢

Here is a very low-key way to get your guests mingling and swapping stories. All you need is a list of pre-prepared questions, so this game couldn't be easier on you wedding organizers!

Your questions could go something like this:

    ✳ Whose birthday is closest to the wedding date?
    ✳ Who is the oldest person here?
    ✳ Who has traveled to the most states?
    ✳ Who owns the most pets?
    ✳ Who has been married the longest?
    ✳ Who has traveled the furthest?
    ✳ Who has met the most famous people?

Make up as many questions as there are centerpieces and award one centerpiece to each person identified by your questions. The more creative you can be with your questions, the better.

Try to choose questions that are unlikely to have many ties. For example, "Who has the most grandchildren?" could have some of your elderly guests fist-fighting for your centerpieces. Questions like "Who traveled the furthest?" are better because you'll get some laughs when all your Danish relatives from the same small town have to figure out who actually had the longer commute to the airport.

For a simpler variation, have only one question and have the winner at each table claim the centerpiece. Questions such as "Who is the youngest person at this table?" or "Who has the oldest car?" work well for this version.

Story Time

Spiciness: ♥
Complexity: 💣
Activity Level: 📢

For some reason, this simple game always gets people really excited. It's a perfect way to create some enthusiasm around winning one of your centerpieces.

Have the youngest person at each table pick up their spoon. Then, the guests must get ready to listen to a wedding story about the bride and groom that includes the words "left" and "right." Whenever one of these words is said, the spoon must be passed to the guest in the corresponding direction.

Invent your own story or use this one (substituting the correct names, of course):

*It was Friday night and Lara was admiring her beautiful wedding dress - it was just **right** for her special day. She had **left** Mike at his best man's house so they wouldn't see each other **right** before the wedding. Mike had wanted to stay at home, but Lara convinced him that she was **right**, as usual!*

*It was getting late, but Lara was too excited for the big day to go **right** to bed, so she **left** her dress in the bedroom and turned **right** to go downstairs to the kitchen to get a drink. Unfortunately, "someone" had **left** his skateboard near the stairs - Lara quickly veered **right** to avoid an accident!*

*Lara thought to herself, Who in their **right** mind would leave a skateboard so close to the stairs? I'm lucky I didn't fall **right** on my bottom! She shook her head slowly from **left** to **right**, **left** to **right**, **left** to **right**... and then went **right** to the kitchen to get that drink.*

*After a glass of wine, all that was **left** was for Lara to get her beauty sleep. She went **right** back upstairs, avoiding the skateboard, and went **right** to bed. Lara **left** a nightlight on because she's afraid of the dark when Mike's not around!*

*The next morning, Lara sprang out of bed – it was her wedding day! She was so excited that she got ready in a hurry and then **left** for the beauty salon. She met her bridesmaids there, who sat to the **left** and **right** of her.*

*Once everyone was suitably primped, they decided to go to the church **right** away. They hopped in the car and turned **right** down the road to the church and then **right** into the church parking lot. Lara entered the bride's room and looked around. Something seemed to be missing!*

*"Oh no!" Lara shouted, realizing her mistake. "I **left** my wedding dress at home!" Lara decided there was no time to find the car, so she **left** the church and ran all the way home. She knew a short cut – she turned **right** out of the parking lot and then **right** into the woods. She ran **right** through the woods and wound up at her house.*

*She bolted upstairs and grabbed her dress. It was **right** where she'd **left** it, in the **right** side of the bedroom closet. Lara rushed **right** back to the church, just in time for the ceremony. All that was **left** was for her to marry the man of her dreams: Mike, her very own Mr. **Right**.*

*And they lived happily ever after... **right**?*

This story works well because it pretty much guarantees that everyone will get to hold the spoon at least once. If you decide to write your own story, make sure it's long enough to include everyone at the table.

Either way, choose a storyteller with a flair for the dramatic. For example, someone who pauses just before the last "right" will make the real winner that much more excited when they get the spoon at the very last second! Also, the story should be read relatively slowly, especially when there are a lot of "lefts" and "rights" in succession. Give people just enough time to fight a little over that spoon!

The person holding the spoon at the end of the story wins the centerpiece at their table. For extra fun, personalize your story by including the names of friends, people in the bridal party, or family members.

Pig Out Piggybank

Spiciness: ⊘
Complexity: 💣💣💣
Activity Level: 🔊

This is a unique game that can help put a little much-needed moolah in the pockets of the bride and groom. There isn't much advanced preparation necessary, but be sure to have some people on standby for the counting part.

Instead of (or in addition to) centerpieces, purchase piggybanks. They don't have to be shaped like piggies, of course! These days you can have everything from plastic clown-shaped banks to gorgeous pewter creations. Choose whatever type of coin bank suits your wedding's theme and color choices.

When the dinner is getting started, announce that you're having a little fundraiser game for the newlyweds. Ask guests to donate their spare change into the coin banks at their respective tables. You should also remind them once or twice throughout the meal, but don't go overboard.

During coffee, collect all the coin banks and solicit the help of some people to count how much money was in each table's bank. Each person at the winning table gets their own coin bank – minus the money, of course!

If you choose to have both coin banks and centerpieces, give the winners one of each or save the centerpieces as prizes for other games.

***Bonus Idea**: Instead of keeping the money for the bride and groom, announce that you're collecting it on behalf of the couple's favorite charity. After the wedding, donate the money in the names of all of the wedding guests, and don't forget to thank them for their kind gesture in the thank-you notes!*

Coloring Contest

Make photocopies of pages 184-187!
(instructions on page 183)

Spiciness: ♥
Complexity: 💣💣
Activity Level: 🔊

Adults seldom admit it (or sometimes they just forget), but they love coloring almost as much as kids do and, like kids, they could usually use a little something to entertain them during those lulls at the dinner table.

This little game is a nod to days gone by when waitresses used to bring you a cup full of crayons to color with on your paper placemat.

Just like the restaurants, this game requires crayons for each table and something to color on. You'll also need some masking tape and a bit of blank wall or some kind of big board (like a portable white board – many reception halls have them).

At the start of dinner, announce that you will be holding a coloring contest throughout the meal. The prizes, of course, are your centerpieces! You can choose the best colorer at each table or simply choose as many winners as you have centerpieces.

To make the contest wedding-related, use coloring book-type pictures of wedding items, such as a wedding dress, bouquet, or wedding cake (see our reproducible pictures and details starting on page 183). Better yet, get caricatures done of the bride and groom and have your guests color them in! In the corner of each picture, remember to leave a spot for guests to fill in their name and table number.

As guests finish their entries, have them come up to the board/wall and tape their picture up for all to see. You could also ask the servers to do this for you. Make sure the pictures are in view of the bride and groom, who will be the coloring contest judges.

Somewhere around the end of the meal, the bride and groom should announce their top picks, congratulate the lucky winners, and tell them they have earned the right to take home a centerpiece. You might also want to save these works of art for the wedding scrapbook!

For a simpler (and potentially funnier) version of this game, put blank pieces of paper on the tables instead of coloring pages and have people draw their best impression of the newlyweds. Remember to have them include their name and table number!

Who's First?

Spiciness: ♥
Complexity: 💣
Activity Level: 📢

Here's a super-easy game to unload your centerpieces. All you need to do ahead of time is think up a "first" for your guests. Centerpieces will be awarded to the "first" person at each table.

Here are some examples:

At each table at the reception:

   ✳ Who was the first person to go to the bathroom?
   ✳ Who was the first person to get dessert?
   ✳ Who was the first person to make the bride and groom kiss?
   ✳ Who was the first person to sit down?

In general:

   ✳ Who was the first person to reply to the wedding invitation?
   ✳ Who was the first person to meet the bride or groom?
   ✳ Who got married first?
   ✳ Who was born first?

For a slightly more complex variation, come up with a different "first" for each table instead of having the same "first" for the whole room. The funnier your "firsts," the better.

Crazy Captions

Spiciness: ♥ to ♥♥♥
Complexity: 💣 💣
Activity Level: 🔊

This game rewards your most creative guests with the centerpieces. Before the reception, find a cute and/or funny photo of the happy couple. Make photocopies of the pictures on regular paper, enough so that each guest has at least one.

Scatter the sheets of paper on the tables and tell guests that their mission is to create the most creative captions possible to go along with the pictures. Remember to tell them that the best caption creators win your centerpieces!

Have as many categories as you have centerpieces. Some ideas are:

* The Funniest
* The Cutest
* The Most Appropriate
* The Most Inappropriate
* The Weirdest
* The Most Factual (i.e. the closest to what actually was said)
* The Most Original

When the guests finish their captions, they should bring them up to the head table. Of course, the bride and groom should be the judges of this contest!

If you've really got a lot of tables at your party, award multiple centerpieces for whichever categories you like best. Alternatively, you could have more than one picture on the tables and give away the centerpieces to the best in each category for each picture.

Name That Tune

Spiciness: ♥
Complexity: 💣💣
Activity Level: 🔊

This classic game is a unique way to give your centerpieces away to the marital music trivia buffs at your wedding. Make sure to have enough slips of paper and pencils for each guest at each table.

Start by making a CD of well-known marriage-related songs, such as:

* Chapel of Love
* Here Comes the Bride
* Love and Marriage
* When I'm 64
* Pachelbel's Canon in D
* Can I Have This Dance?
* Diamonds are a Girl's Best Friend
* L-O-V-E
* White Wedding
* Today I Met the Boy I'm Gonna Marry

You'll want to combine the songs together, with only five or six seconds for each one. If you don't know how to do this, ask a techie friend for help or just make a good old-fashioned mixed tape. The idea is to have about one minute of memorable parts of the above songs.

Announce to your guests that you'll be playing the song clips in succession and that they are to write down as many songs as they can. Play through the song clips twice to give people a fighting chance.

The winner is the person at each table who writes down the most song titles. In case of a tie, award extra points for getting the most songs in the correct order or knowing the most singers of the songs.

Hollywood Weddings

Spiciness: ♥
Complexity: 💣💣
Activity Level: 📢

This game always scores big points at weddings because it's fast-paced, lots of fun, and a great way to give away your centerpieces.

Make sure there are enough sheets of paper and pencils on the tables for each wedding guest. When it's time to give away the centerpieces, tell everyone that you're about to have a contest. Whoever can write down the most unique titles of wedding movies wins a centerpiece.

"Unique title" means that if any two people at a given table write down the same movie name, no point is scored. For example, say Kate and Chuck are sitting at the same table and these are the lists they come up with:

Kate's List:

* ✳ Father of the Bride
* ✳ Wedding Crashers
* ✳ My Best Friend's Wedding
* ✳ Four Weddings and a Funeral
* ✳ Mamma Mia!
* ✳ The Wedding Planner

Chuck's List:

* ✳ Mamma Mia!
* ✳ Runaway Bride
* ✳ The Wedding Singer
* ✳ Four Weddings and a Funeral
* ✳ Father of the Bride
* ✳ Muriel's Wedding

Kate would score one point each for *Wedding Crashers*, *My Best Friend's Wedding*, and *The Wedding Planner* (three points in total). Chuck would get points for *Runaway Bride*, *The Wedding Singer*, and *Muriel's Wedding* (also three points). No one would get points for the other movies because they appeared on more than one person's list.

Set a timer for two minutes and put the tables to work. Let them know that the more movies they can come up with, the better their chances are of winning. Also, encourage creativity. The movies don't need to be all about weddings; any movie with a wedding scene will do.

After two minutes, have each table discuss their lists to see who's got the most points. The winner, of course, gets the centerpiece.

If there is a tie (as with Kate and Chuck), you can award the center-piece to whoever had the longest list of movies, or come up with a sudden-death round: the first person to correctly answer a wedding movie trivia question takes home the prize.

You can also play this game with wedding-related song titles or even wedding vocabulary.

Bonus Idea: *You can play this game at virtually any wedding event - the engagement party, bridal shower, rehearsal dinner, cocktail reception, gift opening... you name it. Give away prizes or just use it as a fun time filler. If you'd like, expand the game by playing more rounds with different wedding themes, such as celebrity couples, popular wedding gifts, or, as mentioned above, wedding songs or wedding vocabulary.*

Bonus Idea: *Make this game bachelorette party-worthy by using spicier categories, such as common (read: bad) pickup lines, types of sex toys, or local bar names.*

Alphabet Action

Spiciness: ♥
Complexity: 💣💣
Activity Level: 📢

This is a very simple game that gives you a cute, no-muss way to divvy up your centerpieces. All you need is a variety of food/candy with letters or words on it and some little dishes to put them in.

The object of this game is for your guests to spell the longest love-related sentence they can using only the food provided. You should give guests such alphabetic options as:

* ✳ alphabet cereal
* ✳ love hearts
* ✳ M&Ms (check the Internet for how to buy customized M&Ms)
* ✳ chocolate hugs and kisses
* ✳ alphabet soup pasta
* ✳ gummi letters

(For more inspiration, do an Internet search for "alphabet candy." You could also use non-food alphabet beads, magnets, or stickers.)

Put one dish of each kind of alphabet food on each table. Tell the guests that they may play throughout the meal and that the centerpieces will be awarded just before the dinner finishes (or whenever you prefer). Each table will play as a team - don't let guests each make their own sentence or you'll have too many to judge!

The bride and groom should decide on the winning table by passing around a microphone and having each table recite their entry. Each guest at the winning table gets a centerpiece to take home!

Wedding Factoids

Make photocopies of page 189!
(instructions and answers on page 188)

Spiciness: ♥
Complexity: 💣
Activity Level: 📢

Wedding Factoids is a unique trivia game that everyone will enjoy. Use our version (see pages 188-189) or do a little research of your own.

This is a multiple-choice game based on wedding traditions. For example, did you know that the reason bridesmaids dress alike and similar to the bride is because in the old days, people thought dressing similarly would confuse the evil spirits so they wouldn't be able to pester the bride? It's true! (At least that's what the Internet says.)

Here's a sample question from the game:

Why do brides carry bouquets?

a. Because the bouquet symbolizes the beauty that the bride will bring to her husband's life.
b. They used to carry fruit, but flowers gradually took over as a result of famines.
c. People wanted to mask the smell of stinky brides.

The answer is... c! Yup, it's true. Back in the days of yore (ah, good old yore), bathing was a luxury. Brides carried fragrant blooms to mask any unseemly odors.

Distribute the quizzes to each person at your reception and tell them that whoever scores the highest at each table will win their centerpiece. At a designated time, collect the quizzes and score them. Award the centerpieces and congratulate the winners on their factoid expertise!

If there are any ties, have a coin toss until you've got just one winner.

Personal Crossword Puzzle

Check out the trivia appendix on page 169!

Spiciness: up to you!
Complexity: 🧨🧨
Activity Level: 🔊

Here's a pencil-and-paper game that is absolutely charming. To prepare, you'll need a computer with Internet access and a printer.

Do an online search for "crossword puzzle generator." These are fabulous websites that allow you to input your own words and hints for a crossword and, with a click of the mouse, the website takes your details and creates you a crossword!

Remember, this is no ordinary crossword puzzle; this is a *personalized* wedding crossword puzzle, so you should use words and names that apply specifically to your wedding. You could use the bride and groom's names, the name of the ceremony location, the honeymoon destination, the flavor of wedding cake, etc. Take a look at our trivia appendix on page 169 for inspiration.

Once your crossword is done, print it and have enough copies made for each of your guests. Plain paper is fine, but consider using paper that matches your color scheme. You could also get the crosswords printed on placemat-sized paper and use them instead of placemats!

Make sure there are enough puzzles and pencils at each table. When everyone is seated for dinner, tell them that the first person at each table to complete their puzzle will win a centerpiece.

Bonus Idea: *Continue with this theme by using crossword place cards and have puzzle books as your wedding favors.*

Bonus Idea: *Keep the completed puzzle of whoever finishes first and frame it. It will be a lovely memento of the fun everyone had at the reception.*

The Reception:

Bouquet/Garter Toss Games

There's nothing terrible about the traditional way of giving away the bouquet and garter, but that doesn't mean there aren't a lot of of fun ways to do it differently!

Sometimes the bouquet is just too delicate to toss through the air. Sometimes the old way to give away the garter is just too racy... and sometimes it's not racy enough!

A few of the games in this section are only for bachelorettes and others are only for bachelors. The remaining games are for both sexes to play together.

Whichever one(s) you choose, you can be sure that your bouquet and garter toss will be events to remember!

You've Got to Fight for Your Right to Maaaaarrrrrry!

Spiciness: ♥
Complexity: 💣💣
Activity Level: 📢 📢 📢

When it's time to give away the garter and bouquet, try this lively game that will make the singles at your wedding work hard for their trophies. This is a great one to slot in near the start of your dance because it really gets people excited to move.

Before the wedding reception, prepare a list of five or six items that some or most of your guests will be likely to have on them. Examples include:

* a $100 bill
* a high-heel shoe
* a stick of gum
* cuff links
* a Blackberry

* a lighter
* a gas station receipt
* a sock
* a pen
* a nail file

When you call up all the singles, get them to bring their chairs with them, but immediately take two away (one from the men, one from the women). Then announce that the singles will be competing for the right to take home the garter/bouquet and they need the help of the rest of the guests.

Next, explain that the competitors will be rushing into the crowd to find the items that will be called out, and then racing back to find a seat. The last man and woman back won't have a chair – they're out.

Begin the game. Enhance the atmosphere by asking your DJ to play some kind of race-like music, such as the "Benny Hill" theme song. Call out the first item on the list and send the contestants running.

When they return, send the last man and woman back to their tables and have them each take a chair with them. Then call the next item. Continue until you've got one winner each for the bouquet and the garter.

To make sure this game goes smoothly, put a good deal of space between the men's and women's chairs, or they're liable to cheat (those little monkeys!). You could also run separate games for the garter and bouquet, although it will take up considerably more time and you'll need to come up with a longer list of items.

If you've got a lot of singles at your wedding, remove more than one chair per round so that people are eliminated faster, and don't forget to return people's items at the end of the game (especially those shoes and $100 bills!).

Super Sexy Belly Dancers

Spiciness: ♥♥♥
Complexity: 💣
Activity Level: 📣 📣

Don't worry – this game doesn't involve spending thousands of dollars importing exotic belly dancers from the Middle East. Little did you know, you've got belly dancing talent right there at your reception.

It's the men! (The single men, to be specific.)

Bring all the single guys up in front of your guests and give them each a silk or chiffon scarf... heck, even a bandana will do in a pinch. Announce that if they want the garter, they'll have to dance for it.

Next comes the crucial step: ask your daring men to expose their bellies. That's right: this isn't just any dance contest – it's a belly dance contest! Make sure you've got some appropriate music ready to go!

The best belly dancer wins the garter. How do you judge who's the winner? That's up to you, of course, but if you've got a lot of singles up there, it's fun to make the bride the judge. If you've only got a handful of dancers, get out your imaginary applause-o-meter and have the guests hoot and clap for the sexiest belly of them all.

If you'd like, pair this game with *Strongest Woman Competition*, on the following page.

Strongest Woman Competition

Spiciness: ♥
Complexity: 💣
Activity Level: 🔊 🔊

When it's time to give away the bouquet, call up all the single ladies. Let them know that you're going to find out which of them is the strongest.

For extra laughs, point out a few very heavy objects nearby, such as speakers, the buffet table, or the wedding cake, and tell the ladies they're going to have to lift them. Better yet, tell the girls that whoever can hold the groom up in the air the longest wins.

You're kidding, of course! All the single ladies have to do is show off their best body builder poses. An energetic host can model a few of the typical poses you'd see in a body building competition. You can have the groom judge or have the audience choose their favorite by their applause.

Play some girl power music and get ready for lots of laughter as your ladies flex and grunt their hearts out! Point out their giant muscles and strained faces, and remember to warn the bachelors out there that these women mean business!

Oh, and don't forget to give the bouquet to the best lady body builder!

This game goes well with *Super Sexy Belly Dancers*, found on the previous page.

Mr. and Mrs. Veggie

Spiciness: ♥
Complexity: ● ● ●
Activity Level: ◀))

Here's a fun contest that promises to get the crowd laughing as your single guests compete for the bouquet and garter.

To prepare for this game, you'll need to purchase a variety of fruits and vegetables. The more colorful and unusual, the better.

Gather the singles together and announce that in order to win the bouquet or garter, they'll have to build their best imitation of the bride or groom using only the produce provided. Have the single ladies build brides and the single men build grooms. You could also have the women build their dream men and the men build their ideal women.

First, have them each choose an item for the body. Have a selection of potatoes, carrots, melons, squash, or whatever you think will work as likenesses of the couple's respective body shapes.

Next, it's time to start decorating. The competitors should have lots of produce to choose from, such as blueberries, sprouts, olives, cherry tomatoes, green onions, and the like. You may also want to provide pipe cleaners, stickers, or other crafty items.

Whatever you choose to provide, make sure you've also got a whole lot of round toothpicks (they're sharper than flat toothpicks) so that people have a way to attach the fruits and veggies to each other. Give them three or four minutes only so the pressure will really be on!

Have the bride and groom be the judges of this contest; the bride will award her bouquet to the best creation from the ladies and the groom will award the garter to the most creative man.

Pin the Bouquet/Garter on the Bride

Spiciness: ♥ ♥
Complexity:
Activity Level:

This spin on the party classic *Pin the Tail on the Donkey* is a light-hearted way to give away the bouquet and garter to the crowd's most coordinated/best guessing single.

Prepare a large picture (either real or hand-drawn) of the bride ahead of time. Make sure she has a free hand and one of her thighs semi-exposed! (Or make it super easy by just drawing a giant stick figure with a picture of the bride's head pasted onto it.)

You'll also need either an easel or tape to put the picture up for the game, as well as a bunch of stickers of garters and bouquets (enough for all the singles at the wedding). You can make these on your computer simply by finding pictures on the Internet that you like and then printing them out on special sticker paper (available at all big box office supply stores). Make sure to number each sticker so your guests will know who actually won!

When it's time to give away the bouquet and the garter, call up all the singles and tell them that instead of just tossing the goods, they're going to have to compete against their fellow singles for their prizes. Hand out the stickers and remind everyone to remember the number on their sticker.

Start with the ladies. Blindfold the first person, spin her around twice, and then point her in the direction of the picture. Have her stick her bouquet sticker wherever she thinks it should go. (The bouquet should go over the bride's hand, as if she were holding it.)

Once that's done, pass the blindfold to the next single. If you've got a lot of people, have a couple of blindfolds and some helpers so the ladies are ready to go. The winner is the lady who gets her bouquet closest to the mark.

Next, it's the single gentlemen's turn who, of course, have the garter stickers. They need to try to stick their garters on the bride's thigh. Again, helpers are good to pass along blindfolds and keep things running smoothly.

When you're finished, award the bouquet to the winning female single and the garter to the winning male single. Don't forget to have your MC or DJ encourage the audience to cheer on the competitors!

If there are really a lot of singles at your wedding, consider having two pictures of the bride so that the male and female singles can all play at the same time.

Limbo Limbo

Spiciness: ♥
Complexity: 💣✳
Activity Level: 🔊 🔊 🔊

Nothing beats a good old-fashioned limbo contest to raise the energy level at any gathering. Why not use this party classic to give away the garter and bouquet?

Of course, all you really need is a limbo stick, but it helps to have some upbeat party music playing in the background. Round up all your singles and announce that the male and female champions of the limbo contest will be awarded the bouquet and garter.

Have all the singles line up and start walking beneath the limbo stick, which can be held up by the bride and groom or whomever you choose. Remember, all contestants have to bend backwards to walk underneath. Have the stick holders be the referees – anyone who falls down or is caught ducking underneath is out.

Once everyone has had a turn, the referees need to lower the stick a little to make the game harder. The last male and female standing are the winners!

Jar—o—Marbles

Spiciness: ♥
Complexity: 💣
Activity Level: 📢

Here's an extremely simple, civil game to give away the bouquet and garter. Use this game if you want to avoid any rowdy catfights or if you've got a crowd of particularly shy singles.

Have two large jars filled with colored marbles. Label one jar "bachelors" and the other "bachelorettes." Make sure you know the number of marbles in each one, because your singles are going to be trying to guess the exact count.

Somewhere close to the end of the dinner, announce that all the singles are invited to come up to examine the jars and guess how many marbles are inside. Of course, the single ladies are guessing the "bachelorettes" jar and the single men are guessing the "bachelors" jar. Remember to tell them that the winners get the bouquet and garter!

Although this is a pretty tame game, you can still build excitement and suspense by having your DJ or MC announce how much time is left until the giveaway. Have he or she give ten-, five-, two-, and one-minute announcements, as well as a ten-second countdown.

At the two-minute announcement, call all the singles up to the jars. Pass around the microphone so that each single can announce their guess. Alternatively, if you've got a large number of singles, have them write their guesses down on pieces of paper along with their names and submit them ahead of time. That way you can announce the winner without a lot of hassle (although you will have to make sure someone is on hand to sort through all the entries in time for the giveaway).

Either way, the person closest to the exact number wins! Award the bouquet and garter to the lucky winners.

Bonus Idea: *Choose marbles that coordinate with your wedding color scheme.*

Bonus Idea: *Use chocolate kisses or some other type of candy instead of marbles. Award the winners the sweets as well as the bouquet and garter!*

Bonus Idea: *Instead of marbles, fill the jars with your wedding favors. After the bouquet and garter have been awarded, place the jars near the exit so your guests can grab their favors as they leave. This idea works especially well for small, unbreakable favors like individually wrapped candies, personalized matchbooks, tins of mints, etc.*

I Knew the Bride When She Used to Rock n' Roll

Spiciness: ♥♥
Complexity: 💣
Activity Level: 📢 📢 📢

This give-away-the-bouquet game is the perfect transition into the dance portion of the evening because it involves music and getting everyone up on the dance floor. No props are necessary, but make sure the DJ has the song "I Knew the Bride (When She Used to Rock n' Roll)" or get a copy prior to the big day.

Have the bride stand in a circle of all the single ladies, bouquet in hand. Play the music and encourage everyone to clap along as the bride takes turns dancing with each one of the single girls. The bouquet goes to whomever the bride chooses. She can select the best dancer, craziest dancer, sexiest dancer, most acrobatic dancer... whatever impresses her the most!

For a different twist, have the bride dance with the garter, not the bouquet, and put her in a circle of the single men. She can award the garter to the bachelor of her choosing!

This game is perfect to couple with *I'm Too Sexy*, on the next page.

I'm Too Sexy

Spiciness: ♥ ♥ ♥
Complexity: 💣
Activity Level: 🔊 🔊 🔊

Here is the counterpart to *I Knew the Bride When She Used Rock n' Roll*, found on the previous page. This garter-giveaway game gets a higher spiciness rating because of the song lyrics and because... well, who knows what your tipsy bachelor guests will do when the music comes on?

Again, make sure your DJ has the song "I'm Too Sexy," or bring it along yourself. All the single men stand in a circle around the groom (who is holding the garter) and take turns dancing with him. The groom awards the garter to whichever of his male friends he thinks is the best dancer.

You can also do the ol' switcheroo by having the groom dance with the bouquet in a circle of your single lady guests. He awards the bouquet to his favorite dancer!

Bonus Idea: *You don't have to play both* I Knew the Bride When She Used to Rock n' Roll *and* I'm Too Sexy. *Some brides prefer to throw their bouquet and then surprise their grooms with this non-traditional way of giving away the garter. (Perhaps this is because she knows he wouldn't agree to it unless he was put on the spot!)*

Newlywed Trivia Competition

Check out the trivia appendix on page 169!

Spiciness: up to you!
Complexity: ●●●
Activity Level: ◁))

Here's another creative way to incorporate trivia into your wedding reception. This time, your single guests need to answer the questions to take home their prizes.

This games gets a pretty high complexity rating because of the preparation required ahead of time, but I promise that this one's worth the work!

Before the reception, get the bride and groom to answer a series of trivia questions. You may not get through all of them during the game, but prepare quite a few, just to be safe. Don't make the questions too easy!

Once you've got the newlyweds' answers, prepare a list of multiple-choice questions. Each one should include two incorrect answers along with the correct answer.

Here's an example:

Where will Paula and George go on their honeymoon?

a. Camping in the mountains
b. To the beautiful islands of Hawaii
c. Backpacking in Europe

Play for the bouquet first. All the single ladies must form a line and prepare to answer some tricky trivia questions about the happy couple. Have the ladies shout out the answer they think is correct (a, b, or c). Whoever gets the question wrong must return to their seats.

The ladies who answer correctly can proceed to the next question. Yes, this game works more or less on the honor system, but who's going to cheat at a wedding?

Continue until you're down to one winner. If you need to have a tie-breaker, award the bouquet to the lady who shouts out the answer first.

Next, gather up the men and play again to give away the garter. Alternatively, just have all the singles play together and give away their awards when you're down to one man and one woman.

Macarena Match

Spiciness: ♥
Complexity: 💣💣
Activity Level: 📢 📢 📢

Here's a game to test your singles' coordination as well as their ability to win the garter or bouquet with pure, unadulterated luck.

Bring all your singles onto the dance floor and announce that they will have to "Macarena" their way through a series of questions to win the prizes. The last male and female dancers standing will be the winners!

First, teach your singles the Macarena. It's very helpful (and hilarious) to have some kids come up to help out. They should remain throughout the game so the adults have someone to follow.

Come up with a series of questions like:

* Who has (or had!) blond hair?
* Who is wearing blue?
* Who was born in a foreign country?
* Who had the fish (instead of the chicken)?
* Who likes white cake more than chocolate cake?
* Who isn't wearing any jewelry?

Start the music and have your DJ ask the first question. Anyone to whom the question applies must leave the dance floor (e.g. all blonds must sit down). Keep asking questions until you are down to one single man and one single woman. Award them the garter and the bouquet.

You may want to rig the game so that when you're down to only two men or women, you think up a question on the spot that eliminates one of them. This prevents the game from going on forever because – let's be serious – no one wants to listen to the Macarena for an hour!

Everything but the Kitchen Sink

Spiciness: up to you!
Complexity: 🎇🎇🎇
Activity Level: 📣 📣

This game only works if the bride's dress has a long, full skirt. Ahead of time, you should gather about five silly objects and put them in a box.

When it's time to give away the garter, put the box under the chair that the bride will be sitting on. Make sure no one sees you do this! It's a good idea to cut one of the sides of the box off so that the groom can reach into it easily.

Gather the single men together. Have your MC announce, "Okay, Andrew, time to remove Danielle's garter!" Start playing some sexy garter music, but instead of the garter, have the groom pull out an item from the box. Your MC should act surprised and announce what it is.

For example, the groom pulls out a cell phone. The MC could say, "Hmm... a good place to keep a cell phone, but not exactly what we're looking for, Andrew!" Andrew tries again, but this time gets a box of tissues. The MC says, "Okay, it's very common for brides to get emotional on their wedding day, but we're still after that garter!" Next, it's a blow-up guitar, followed by a stash of candy bars...

Finish up by finally removing the bride's garter. Then, tell the single men that the first person to name all the items that were removed from the bride in the correct order will take home the garter (or, of course, you can just do an ordinary garter toss).

Obviously, the key to this game – both for the single men and for the overall humor factor – is the element of surprise. Only the bride, groom, and MC should be in on it. Done correctly, this is one game that promises peals of laughter from your guests!

The Reception:

Games for the Dance

Getting your dance going is not always the easiest thing in the world.

Keeping it going can be even harder.

The #1 most important thing you can do to ensure the success of your dance is hire the right DJ. Choose someone with a lot of experience and positive, current references.

The second most important thing you can do is incorporate a few crowd-pleasing games to encourage people to get up - and stay - on the dance floor.

All of these games can be run by your DJ, so you won't have a thing to do on the big day but relax and enjoy the party with your guests!

You Think You Can Dance?

Spiciness: ♥ ♥
Complexity: 💣 💣 💣
Activity Level: 📢 📢 📢 📢

Yes, this game takes quite a bit of planning ahead of time since it involves making up and memorizing a dance routine, but surprisingly, coordination is not required. For some strange reason, the less coordinated the dancers are, the more your guests will love this game!

Before the reception, the bride and groom need to come up with a dance routine, preferably one to two minutes in length. You may also want to include the wedding party for moral support (and extra laughs!).

Again, dance skills are not a prerequisite for this game. If you need some inspiration, though, think of movies or music videos with awesome dance scenes, such as:

* Thriller
* Footloose
* Flashdance
* Grease
* Saturday Night Fever
* Bring It On

This is a surprising and super high-energy way to transition from the couple's first dance, the father-daughter dance, etc. into the rest of the evening that includes all your guests on the dance floor.

Make sure to have your DJ encourage people to cheer and clap along to the couple's killer moves! At the end of the routine, you may want to keep the music going and send the dancers into the crowd to bring more people up onto the dance floor. Whatever you decide, make sure the DJ plays something upbeat to keep the energy up!

Count the Kisses

Spiciness: ♥
Complexity: 💣☀
Activity Level: 🔊

This game should be played either at the start of the dance or right after some event that interrupts the dance, such as the cake-cutting – this is because it brings everyone up on the dance floor but isn't a dancing game per se. For this one, you'll need a bucketful of chocolate kisses, a willing bride and groom, and wedding guests with very rudimentary math skills.

Have the guests gather around the bride and groom and announce that the bride is going to place as many kisses on her new husband as he can handle.

The groom must remain on his feet but can otherwise be manipulated however the bride sees fit. For example, she'll be able to balance a lot more chocolates on his arms if they're extended out to the side! She can also pile them in his hands, on his head and shoulders, on top of his shoes, on the frames of his glasses, or wherever else she finds a good spot. No pockets allowed, though!

Make sure to have some fun music playing in the background (such as "Steal My Kisses"). Have the guests cheer on the bride and count the kisses as each one is successfully balanced on the groom. When the groom reaches his max, allow guests to come and steal the kisses off of the groom. It's even sweeter to pass out the remaining kisses to all guests on the dance floor or use them as small prizes for other dance games.

Bonus Idea: *Have your chocolate kisses personalized with your monogram for that extra special touch. Just do an Internet search to see how easy it is!*

Dance—o—Rama

Spiciness: ♥
Complexity: 💣💣
Activity Level: 📢 📢 📢

Okay, listen: I *know* that you don't like the Chicken Dance and, as Lord and Lady of the proceedings, you technically have the right to ask your DJ not to play it.

However, before you make a decision, you should know that group dance games are absolutely the number one DJ trick for jam-packing a dance floor, and they really work. Every cheesy song that makes people dance like idiots will be requested by at least ten of your guests and, if you kibosh them all ahead of time, your DJ will have no choice but to blame it all on you.

This doesn't mean that your whole dance should be full of lame-o songs, but try to remember that a rockin' dance is not about playing the music that only the couple loves. It's about keeping a full dance floor with the right combination of a wide variety of songs. It really and truly is an art.

Okay, my rant's over. Now for the songs:

* The Macarena
* The Locomotion
* The YMCA
* The Electric Slide
* The Cha Cha Slide
* The Chicken Dance (did I mention that one already?)
* Hokey Pokey
* Fishin' in the Dark
* Cadillac Ranch
* Beer Barrel Polka
* Time Warp
* Bunny Hop
* Grease Megamix
* The Twist
* Let's Twist Again
* Boot Scootin' Boogie
* The Hustle

If your DJ isn't familiar with any of these songs, don't hire him. Trust me. A good DJ knows all these favorites and more, and also brings along a bunch of prizes to give away during each of them.

For the neophytes, however, here is a quick run-down:

"The Locomotion" and "Bunny Hop" involve people forming a chain by holding onto each other's shoulders or hips. Have them snake throughout the hall and pick up any stragglers who have yet to make it to the dance floor. Give the leader of each chain a funny hat, a lei, or a glow ring.

"Beer Barrel Polka," "Grease Megamix," "The Twist," and "Let's Twist Again" don't really have set games or routines, but they are guaranteed to get people on the floor. It's always a good idea to have a polka or twist contest, or pit male and female guests against each other as they sing their respective parts of the "Grease Megamix."

The remaining songs on the list are all pre-choreographed group or line dances. If you don't know the steps, just ask your DJ or look on the Internet (oh man, does YouTube have some hilarious videos!). It's a good idea to have your DJ or another savvy person lead the actual dance so people can follow someone and learn as they go.

For prizes, have a bunch of small giveaways ready. Ask your DJ company beforehand – many supply these items as part of your package. Alternatively, hand out raffle tickets as prizes and then at the end of the night, call a winning number and give that person a bigger prize.

Song Speedup

Spiciness: ♥
Complexity: 💣
Activity Level: 📢 📢 📢

Before you decide on this game, check with your DJ to make sure their CD player has the ability to speed up and slow down songs manually. (They should, unless they have completely primitive equipment.)

Choose one of the party songs from *Dance-o-Rama* (the previous game) that most of your guests will be familiar with, such as "Let's Twist Again" or the "Hokey Pokey." Tell them that in order to win prizes, they'll have to keep up to the tempo of the song. Have your DJ play up how hard it's going to be and how your guests are really going to have to work for this one.

Then start the song out really slow – this should give everyone a little chuckle. Once people are showing off their best slow-motion moves, the DJ should start increasing the tempo of the song. Keep speeding the song up gradually until it's so fast that your guests look absolutely ridiculous.

Give away prizes close to the end of the song to the guests who are doing their best to keep up. Don't worry about selecting an actual winner – just congratulate everyone for sticking it out!

Pass the Bubbles

Spiciness: ♥
Complexity: 💣
Activity Level: 📢 📢 📢

It's true: adults love bubbles almost as much as kids do. For this game, you'll need about a half dozen mini bubble blowing favors. There are lots of varieties out there specifically for weddings, so you can choose the ones you like best.

This game should follow a popular party song or a slow song, when there are already a lot of people on the dance floor. When you're ready to play, hand out your bubbles randomly to guests already up to dance. Make sure your DJ plays some fun, fast-paced party music!

The rules are simple: if you're holding a bubbles favor, you must blow some bubbles once and then pass the favor onto another guest. When the music stops, whoever is holding the bubbles gets a small prize.

Have a bunch of fun prizes on hand for the winners of this game. You don't need anything too elaborate, just a token to celebrate their luck! Alternatively, give away raffle tickets as prizes and then draw a winner for a bigger prize later on.

Bonus Idea: Play this game to give away your centerpieces. Give one bubbles favor to one person at each table and play some music. That person blows some bubbles once and then passes the bubbles on. When the music stops, the person holding the bubbles wins the centerpiece!

You could also play this as an elimination game where the person holding the bubbles is out and you keep playing until you've got only one person left: the winner of the centerpiece.

Diva Extraordinaire

Spiciness: ♥♥
Complexity: 💣
Activity Level: 📢 📢 📢

There are some party songs that people just can't help but sing along to. Why not exploit this fact in order to poke a little fun at your wedding guests?

When the dance is in full swing, play one of those highly singable songs. Here are some ideas:

* Paradise by the Dashboard Light
* Billie Jean
* Ballroom Blitz
* Bohemian Rhapsody
* My Sharona
* Brown Eyed Girl

Without telling your guests, ask your DJ to survey the crowd and find the craziest, loudest, kookiest guest on the floor "performing" the song. When it's over, award the singer a novelty crown (à la Burger King) and proclaim him or her "Diva Extraordinaire!"

For some extra chuckles, have a few smaller prizes on hand as well. Give those prizes out to people who are still sitting at their tables but were definitely singing along. Dub them "Divas in Training."

If you've got a pretty rowdy crowd, you could organize this game a little more and turn it into a mini air band contest. Choose contestants ahead of time and provide them with those ridiculous inflatable instruments. Give the inflatables away to the winning air band!

Chug! Chug!

Spiciness: ♥
Complexity: ◆
Activity Level: 📢 📢

Use this game as a brief interlude to your dance festivities. All you need is your DJ and as many cans of soda as you have contestants.

Ask three or more of your guests to participate in this game. Include a child for extra laughs (because they'll probably win). Give each one of them a can of soda and tell them that whoever finishes it first will win a prize. No cheating now - don't let anyone open the can until the contest has officially begun!

To enhance the excitement, ask people to cheer for whom they think will win beforehand, and have your DJ play some upbeat, fast-tempo music. When everyone is sufficiently ramped up, shout, "On your marks, get set, go!"

Award the fastest drinker a gag prize like an anti-gas medicine, a six-pack of the soda they just chugged, or a *Guinness Book of World Records* (with the "longest burp" page earmarked).

Musical Laps

Spiciness: ♥ ♥
Complexity: 💣
Activity Level: 📢 📢 📢

Don't worry; this game isn't nearly as dirty as it sounds. *Musical Laps* is a twist on musical chairs that guarantees to have people chuckling and possibly landing in heaps on the floor.

Like regular musical chairs, you should start out with enough chairs for all but one player. Start the music and let people dance around the chairs. When the music stops, everyone must find a seat, including the person who doesn't have a chair. That means he or she must share a chair with someone else.

For round two, play the music and take away a chair. When the music stops again, same deal: everyone must find a seat. Continue in this manner, taking away an extra chair every time you start the music again. Get ready for lots of giggles as more and more people attempt to balance on progressively fewer chairs!

If you've got a lot of players, it's smart to have two or three games going at once. Give prizes to the team who can balance the most people on the fewest chairs without toppling over!

Ring Toss

Spiciness: ♥
Complexity: 💣💣
Activity Level: 🔊 🔊

Here is a bride versus groom challenge to up the energy level at your dance. You will need some kind of rings and some kind of "pegs." I recommend glow rings (everyone loves glow rings!) and cans of soda or bottles of beer.

In this game, the bride must team up with her maid of honor and the groom with his best man. The "pegs" can be placed on the floor, but putting them on small tables is better because it makes it easier for your guests to see what's going on and it involves much less bending down. The bride and groom each have their own peg.

Have the bride and groom stand a set distance away from their respective pegs with their teammates waiting by the pegs. The object of the game is to toss the ring onto the peg as many times as possible in two minutes. After the bride tosses the ring towards her peg, her maid of honor tosses it back to her so she can keep playing, and likewise with the groom and best man. In addition, the maid of honor and best man should keep track of their team's score.

When the game begins, the host should have people cheer on the bride and groom. Also have him announce when there are only 60, 30, and 20 seconds left, and then do a ten-second countdown.

Let the winning team choose their prizes: either the glow rings, whatever you used for the pegs, or one of each. Give the remaining two prizes to the losers.

Make sure your DJ follows up with a high-energy song that will entice all the onlookers to stay on the floor and shake their tail feathers!

Dance Olympics

Spiciness: ♥
Complexity: ●●●
Activity Level: ◁)) ◁)) ◁))

This game requires virtually no preparation but can be fairly difficult to compete in, so it earns three points for both complexity and activity level. The laughter from both spectators and competitors will make it well worth it, though.

Have males and females pair off and tell them that they're about to compete in the *Dance Olympics*, a test of both strength and stamina. The Olympic events are as follows:

Men's kneel	Men get down on one knee; women sit on their knee. Only one of her feet can touch the floor.
Ladies' kneel	Women get down on one knee; men sit on their knee. Only one of his feet can touch the floor.
Men's piggy back	Men piggy back their ladies. No body parts can be on the floor except for the men's feet and hands.
Ladies' piggy back	Ladies piggy back their men. No body parts can be on the floor except for the women's feet and hands.
Men's cradle	Men hold their women so that no part of her is touching the floor.
Ladies' cradle	Women hold their men so that no part of him is touching the floor.

When the music is playing, the competing couples dance together. When the music stops, the DJ must call out one of the Olympic event names and everyone must get into the proper position. Anyone who either does the wrong position or can't hold the position is out.

If these Olympic events will be too difficult for your guests to manage in their wedding attire, simplify them by choosing less complicated positions. Here are some easier examples:

* Make the shapes of letters with your bodies. (Choose letters on the fly or let them spell out the couple's names.)
* Freeze in your current position.
* Balance on one foot (specify left or right).

In any case, continue the game, eliminating couples as you go. If you've got too many die-hards left on the floor, increase the difficulty by making them hold the poses for longer or have them carry their teammates from one side of the dance floor to the other.

When you're down to three couples, award them with bronze, silver, and gold medals. Base your first, second, and third choices on who worked the hardest, looked the funniest, was the most creative, etc. You could also just play for a set amount of time (say the length of one song) and give prizes to those remaining once the game is over.

Nab the Newlywed

Check out the trivia appendix on page 169!

Spiciness: ♥
Complexity: 💣💣💣
Activity Level: 📢📢

Nab the Newlywed is an inventive way to give away the most sought-after prize at the reception: a dance with the bride and groom.

This game is a bit complex because you'll need to prepare trivia questions ahead of time with multiple-choice answers for each. Use the trivia appendix on page 169 to give you inspiration and save you time!

Have your DJ announce that guests will have the chance to compete for a dance with the bride or groom. All guests who'd like to try for the bride go to one side of the dance floor; all guests who'd like to dance with the groom go to the other. The bride and groom must be on the *opposite* side of the floor from their group of contestants.

Now, the DJ reads the first trivia question. Here's a sample:

Who usually makes breakfast on the weekend?

a. The groom does - scrambled eggs and bacon.
b. The bride does - pancakes with warm maple syrup.
c. They each fend for themselves - usually cereal or toast.
d. No one! They eat the leftovers from last night's dinner.

The guests call out their answers and everyone who gets it right may take one big step forward (toward their target); everyone else must stay put. (It gets funny when opposite teams meet in the middle of the dance floor and have to sidestep each other!)

The next question is read and the game continues until the bride and groom have each been reached by a guest. Then it's time for the lucky winners to claim their prize, so cue the music!

Dance Floor Swap

Spiciness: ♥
Complexity: 💣
Activity Level: 📢 📢 📢

This is one of the simplest ways to fill a dance floor. You could try this game near the beginning of the dance (after the newlyweds' and parents' dances), or play it during a lull in the evening when you need to get the energy back up.

Have the DJ announce that it's time for the *Dance Floor Swap* and he needs the bride and groom up on the dance floor. Give the bride and groom identifying props, like neon glow necklaces, bandanas, or funny hats. When the music starts, the couple must start dancing.

When the DJ shouts, "Switch!" the bride and the groom must go into the crowd and each bring a new person up to the floor to dance with. Now there will be two couples on the floor: the bride and her partner and the groom and his partner.

When the DJ shouts, "Switch!" again, these pairs must split up and each of the four people must bring up their own new partners. The game continues like so until the dance floor is pretty much full. Don't play until absolutely everyone is up, though, because you might have an odd number (i.e. someone will be left out) or the last stragglers still sitting at the end may get hurt feelings. Simply have the DJ end the game at an appropriate time and invite everyone else to the floor.

Whether you choose a fast or slow song for this game, make sure it is followed by an up-tempo song that everyone knows and likes (think "Old Time Rock n' Roll" or "Stayin' Alive"). The whole point of this game is to bring people up onto the floor and keep them there!

If the happy couple isn't available, feel free to use another pair to start off, such as the parents, grandparents, or other newlyweds.

The Reception:

Especially for Kids

Even if you've only got a few little tikes at your reception, you (and their parents) will appreciate your having planned a bit of entertainment aimed specifically at kids.

Ask one of the teens at your reception if they'd run these games or, better yet, hire a babysitter for the evening. You should also have plenty of coloring books and crayons handy for quieter kids who just want to hang out and color.

These games were all crafted to be able to include children of all ages simultaneously. In fact, don't be surprised if you even have some "big kids" joining in on the fun!

These games are also adaptable to any environment (just in case you aren't holding your reception in a daycare or on a playground). About half of them will even work right at the dinner table.

Not all of these games are wedding-themed, but don't worry - your youngest guests will still have a ball!

Wink Assassin

Spiciness: ⊘
Complexity: 💣
Activity Level: 📢

This game is the absolute best. I mean it! I loved it when I was a kid, I love it now, and I'd have played it along with the kids at my own wedding if I hadn't had to be there for the cake cutting and first dance and stuff.

Have all the kids sit in a circle and close their eyes (no peeking!). The leader of the game walks around the outside of the circle and gently taps one child on the back once. That person is the assassin. Next, the leader taps another child on the back twice. That person is the detective. The game leader should walk all the way around the circle at least once so the kids sitting down don't have any idea who gets chosen (except the assassin and the detective, of course).

Next, everyone opens their eyes and the kid who is the detective should say so. Then it's time for the assassin to start assassinating which, in this game, is done with a wink. Anyone who gets winked at must lay down – and the more melodramatic the death, the better. (If not all your kids can wink, you can change the game to "Double-Blink Assassin.")

It's the detective's job to try to figure out who the assassin is before everyone dies. When he or she figures it out, start the game again with a new detective and assassin. You can keep playing this game till everyone gets sick of it, which literally might be never ever.

Wedding Draw

Spiciness: ⊘
Complexity: 💣💣💣
Activity Level: 📢

Here's a classic game that is excellent to play with kids of all ages. Don't be surprised if you even snag an adult or two!

For this game, you'll need an easel, some sort of timer, crayons, and a few dozen cards with wedding words on them, such as "cake," "dress," "honeymoon," etc.

Split the kids into two or three teams. There must be at least two people on each team, but more is better. The first team selects a person to go to the easel and draw. That person stands up, takes a card, and then has 30 seconds to draw. The object is to get the children on his team to say the word on the card. The person drawing cannot speak; he can only draw!

Make sure the other children aren't trying to shout out the answer. Only the team who's drawing should be guessing during the 30 seconds. If they guess correctly within the time frame, they get a point.

If the team doesn't guess correctly, the other teams have an opportunity to steal the point. Start with the team to the left of the drawing team. If they know the answer, award them the point; if not, go to the next team. If no one guesses, announce what the word was and then move on to the next team.

Once the team has finished their turn, it's time for the next team to play. Keep playing until one team reaches a certain number of points or until you run out of cards.

There are several variations on this game. For example, you can let teams who guess correctly choose another card and continue playing until they can't guess one correctly. If you play this way, make sure you've got some tougher words on those cards and also have the teams evenly distributed in terms of age and ability so one team doesn't monopolize the whole game.

Another variation is to have speed rounds. Give teams two minutes to successfully draw and guess as many cards as possible. Whoever guesses the most wins!

One more variation is to do away with teams altogether and have all the kids guess while one of them draws. Don't worry about a time limit - the first kid to guess the drawing correctly is the next one to draw.

Bonus Idea: *You can also play this one at your engagement party, bridal shower, bachelorette party, or gift opening. It's definitely not for kids only - although the kids will probably be way better at it!*

Round and Round

This game tests coordination and is guaranteed to keep kids giggling!

Have everyone sit in a circle and place their hands on the floor in front of them, palms down. Then have everyone take their right hand and cross it over the left hand of the person to their right. The result should be a circle of palms-down hands with no one having both of their own hands next to one another. (See the diagram, below.)

Here's how the game works: One hand tap means "keep going in the same direction." Two hand taps (in rapid succession) means "switch directions."

So, let's say you've got Peggy, Erin, Jan, and Spencer sitting in a circle. Their hands would be arranged like this:

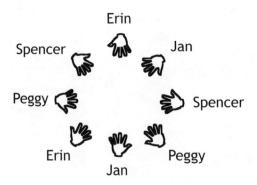

(Bear with me; this game is much easier to play than it is to explain!)

So if Jan starts with her left hand (at the bottom of the diagram on the opposite page) and taps once, it goes to Peggy's right hand (counter-clockwise). Then Peggy taps once and it's on to Spencer's left hand. He taps once, then it's Jan's right hand's turn. Jan taps her right hand twice, so it's back to Spencer's left hand (clockwise). He taps once, so it's Peggy's turn. Peggy taps twice so it's back to Spencer's left hand.

... and so on and so on.

If someone taps at the wrong time, they're out. If someone takes too long to figure out what hand to tap, they're out too. Play until you're down to three or four kids and then give them prizes. Better yet, have the eliminated kids start their own game so no one's left out.

Who's the Leader?

Spiciness: ⊘
Complexity: 🌑
Activity Level: 📢

Here's another simple circle-type game to keep the kids having fun at the reception.

First, seat everyone in a circle. Then, send one child out of the room for a minute. He or she is "it." While "it" is gone, choose someone in the circle to be the leader.

The leader is in charge of starting some kind of movement that everyone in the circle must imitate (such as snapping, clapping hands, slapping the floor, etc.). Once everyone's going with the movement, bring "it" back into the room to rejoin the circle.

At some point, the leader must change the movement and everyone else must follow suit. From where the "it" child is sitting, he or she must guess who is leading the movements by figuring out who's changing their movements first.

When the leader is spotted, send that child out of the room and start another round.

Untie the Knot

Spiciness: ⊘
Complexity: 💣
Activity Level: 📢 📢

They all saw the bride and groom tie the knot – now it's time to untie a knot! This game requires absolutely no preparation and is perfect for kids of all ages to play together.

Have all the children stand in a small circle and close their eyes. Now, they must reach into the middle of the circle and grab any two people's hands. It's best if they aren't holding the hands of the people next to them and if each child is holding the hands of two different people. It *will* work no mater how they latch onto one another, but feel free to do a little rearranging after the kids have opened their eyes again.

Now all the kids have to do is untangle themselves without letting go of each other's hands. They'll have to step over and under each other's arms and twist around each other, but it is always 100% possible to untie this human knot!

This game encourages lots of giggles and getting-to-know-you time. Don't be surprised if everyone wants to play five or six times! However, if you have any children who don't want to play, ask them to be the helpers. It can be good to have an outside pair of eyes trying to figure out the best way to untie the knot.

Bonus Idea: *Play this game with the guests at your bridal shower or bachelorette party, as well. It's an instant icebreaker!*

Shoe Showdown

Spiciness: ⊘
Complexity: 💣
Activity Level: 🔊 🔊 🔊

This active game is sure to garner some giggles from your youngest wedding guests. All you need for this game are some kids and their shoes!

Have all the children remove their shoes and throw them into a pile. Get them to close their eyes and then mix up their shoes a little so they won't know exactly where their own shoes are.

To play, the children need to open their eyes and find their shoes. Once they've found them, they must put their shoes on and race to a designated place in the room and back.

Instead of having this game have one winner and a whole bunch of losers, play this game as a relay, so only one child at a time searches for his or her shoes. Tell the kids that they all have to get back with their shoes on by a set time (one minute or so) and if they can do it, they'll all win some candy or a party favor of some sort. (You should probably rig your timing so that they win by the second or third play.)

Camouflage

Spiciness: ⊘
Complexity: 💣
Activity Level: 📢 📢

This is a hide-and-seek type of game with a twist. The child who's "it" must stand in a designated spot and can't move for the entire time they're "it." They can, however, rotate freely on the spot they've chosen.

"It" closes their eyes and counts to 20 to give all the other kids time to hide. The catch is that the hiders must choose spots from which they can see "it" at all times, even if they've only got one little eyeball peeking out. The theory is that if the hiders can see "it," then "it" must also be able to (eventually) spot the hiders.

"It" must look around and try to figure out where everyone is hidden. They don't have to call the children by name – they can just name the hiders' locations once they identify where someone is. The last child to be found is the next to be "it."

If "it" is having a hard time spotting hiders, have the child choose one direction to look and freeze that way. Then, tell the hiders that everyone must reveal their location for just one second. Once that's finished, "it" can call out any hiders they've discovered and can then move again.

1–2 Switch!

Spiciness: ⊘
Complexity: 💣
Activity Level: 📢 📢 📢

For this game you'll need as many chairs as you have children, minus one. Give every chair a number – it's good if you can write the numbers on pieces of paper and then tape them to the backs of the chairs. Make sure the chairs are spread out far enough so the kids have a little room to run.

Have the kids arrange their chairs in a circle. The child without a chair stands in the middle. The middle child then calls out two numbers and the kids who are sitting in those chairs must try to exchange places. At the same time, the middle child is trying to steal either one of the chairs from the two kids who are running to the opposite seats. Whoever is left standing calls the two numbers for the next round.

This game gets funny when the kids have switched seats a couple of times and can't quite remember which chair is which. If you've got an especially clever group of munchkins, reorder the chairs periodically so the children (including the middle child) have a tougher time figuring out who is sitting at which number.

If you have a very large group of kids, have the middle person call out three numbers or more so the game moves a little more quickly.

If this game is too difficult for your group of kids, just have them call out each other's names. This is also a good way to help the kids get to know one another.

Two Truths and a Lie

Spiciness: ⃠
Complexity: 💣
Activity Level: 📢

This game works well as a wind-down game or a game to play while kids are eating, recovering from a super active game, or when you're just expected to keep them quiet.

All the kids have to do is think of three things about themselves to tell the rest of the group. Two of these things must be true and one must be a lie. Encourage the kids to be as creative as they can.

When everyone's ready, select one child to start. Once all three statements have been spoken, the first person to correctly guess which one is the lie gets to go next.

Some kids will want multiple turns, especially if they weren't able to trick anyone into thinking their lie was true on their first turn. Some kids might be too shy to play, but don't worry - they'll enjoy just being spectators.

Keep playing until you're ready to move on to another activity.

Robot Race

Spiciness: ⊘
Complexity: 💣
Activity Level: 📢 📢

This game is perfect if you don't have a ton of space for kids to run around without disturbing the other guests.

Set start and finish lines for the race. Put kids in groups of two or three. One kid on each team must be the robot; the other kids are the scientists. Tell the scientists that they must get their robots across the finish line, but the robots cannot move at all because their batteries have died.

Tell all the children that the robots must have one foot on the floor at all times. To play, children will have to physically pick up and move the legs of their robots while making sure that they don't knock their robots over!

Have various types of candy or small toys for prizes. Let first place choose their prizes first, second place choose their prizes second, and so on until everyone's got a prize.

Marshmallow Cake Makers

Spiciness: ⊘
Complexity: 💣💣
Activity Level: 📢

For this game, you'll need a lot of marshmallows of various colors and sizes. It's also a good idea to have toothpicks and scissors for the children who are old enough to use them without hurting themselves.

Tell the children that their mission is to build the most beautiful wedding cake they can using only marshmallows. Toothpicks will help provide stability and scissors are for extra creative freedom. You could also provide fine-point markers so kids can actually decorate individual marshmallows themselves.

If you only have a few kids, let them work on their own. Otherwise, have them work in pairs or groups of three. Don't make the groups too large or some kids may feel that their creative vision is being stifled!

Award certificates for various categories, such as the prettiest cake, the tastiest-looking cake, the tallest cake, the craziest cake, the most creative, etc. Make sure everyone gets an award!

If this finishes too quickly or you have leftover marshmallows, have the kids make the prettiest marshmallow wedding dress or the handsomest marshmallow groom.

You could also vary this game by providing other similar candies, like marshmallow strawberries and bananas, Marshmallow Peeps, and Gummi Bears.

Other Events:

Bridal Shower Games

Bridal showers are the perfect way to get together with the girls and have a little fun before the big day, but some of the games for this time-honored event are a little tired.

This section includes brand new shower games, as well as a few new-and-improved versions of old classics, to get your ladies mingling, giggling, and having a wonderful time.

Most of these games work as well with men as with women, so you can also use them at a couple's shower or engagement party.

These games all include small prizes for your guests because, hey, why should the bride be the only one getting all the presents? They will also work to give away your bridal shower centerpieces, if you have them.

How to Be a Good Wife

Make photocopies of pages 191-192!
(instructions on page 190)

Spiciness: ♥
Complexity: 💣
Activity Level: 📢

Here's a quirky one to get the conversation flowing at your shower. It's a quiz based on a home economics textbook from the 1950s. Your guests won't believe how far wives have come in just a few decades!

Take the following question, for example:

How should you react if your husband stays out all night?

a) Freak out, demand details, and make him sleep on the sofa for a week.
b) Explain how worried you were and that in the future, you'd prefer a phone call.
c) Just be glad you've got a husband at all and don't ask questions.
d) Listen to his explanation patiently and then decide how to react.

If you guessed something sensible, you are incorrect! The housewife of the '50s would do no less than (c) for her man. Seriously. (To check out the whole excerpt, do an Internet search for "how to be a good wife 1950.")

You can do your own research to make up a quiz, or just make photocopies of pages 191-192. As you pass the quiz around to your guests, tell them that it's based on marriage advice from the 1950s and to answer how they think a good wife of that era should respond.

Not only will the quiz really loosen up your guests and get them chatting, but it's also a great opportunity to give away some cute prizes. Think era-appropriate goodies such as vintage lunch pails, polka dot purses, or sillier items like hairnets or rubber gloves.

Tray of Trinkets

Spiciness: up to you!
Complexity:
Activity Level:

Here's a fairly straightforward game that will require your guests to use their noodles.

Before the party, prepare a tray of about two dozen small items. You could include both tame and spicy things, such as the following:

* a tube of lipstick
* salt and pepper shakers
* a condom
* underwear
* a key
* a bottle of aspirin
* pantyhose

* a strand of pearls
* a fork
* toothpaste
* a bottle of lotion
* a deck of cards
* a kazoo
* novelty handcuffs
* a hairbrush

Give all of your guests pieces of paper and pens. Then, bring the tray out covered with a cloth or towel. Tell your guests that they are going to try to remember as many items as they can from the tray. They will have one minute to look at the tray, but they can't write anything down during that time.

When the time's up, hide the tray's items and tell the guests to get writing. Have prizes for whoever can remember the most items. Make sure you've got some backup goodies on hand in case there is a tie.

For extra fun, use some of the tray items as prizes. For example, you could purchase novelty handcuffs, a nice bottle of lotion, or even a vibrator (woohoo!). Use them for the game and then award them to the first, second, and third place winners.

Build-a-Cake

Spiciness: ⊘
Complexity: 💣💣
Activity Level: 📢

This game is a creative way to get your bridal shower guests working together and definitely sharing a giggle or two!

To prepare for this game, have a bunch of crafty items available, such as construction paper, markers, scissors, wrapping paper, glitter, stickers, pipe cleaners, sequins, glue, and a variety of empty boxes (such as cereal, cardboard, or tissue boxes).

Start the game by explaining to your guests that your fiancé didn't want to splurge on a wedding cake, so instead they're going to have to make one for you!

If you'd like, you can divide your guests into several teams and have them compete to make the most imaginative cake. You can award bonus points to the team that builds the tallest cake or manages to make a little bride and groom for the top.

Once the cakes are finished, reward your guests by serving a real cake. You might also want to consider showcasing their artwork at your reception!

Pass the Parcel

Spiciness: ♥
Complexity: 💣💣
Activity Level: 📢

Here's a nice sit-down game to play while you're enjoying coffee or dessert. Start by purchasing a nice gift, like a candle, blank journal, or some fuzzy slippers.

Next, wrap the gift, but not just once or twice. Wrap it a couple of dozen times and between each layer, put other, smaller gifts, such as temporary tattoos, little chocolate bars, sticks of gum, travel-sized lotions, individual gourmet hot chocolate packets, and the like.

To play, have some music playing. Your guests pass the package around until the music stops. Whoever is holding the package at that point gets to unwrap a layer and keep the present they find between the layers. When the music starts again, continue passing the package. The game goes on until the last person unwraps the bigger gift at the center of the package.

Bonus Idea*: Spice up this game by including truth or dare questions on slips of paper in between the layers, instead of little gifts.*

Bonus Idea*: Put "get to know you" questions on slips of paper between the layers along with the small gifts. This is especially appropriate if many of your bridal shower attendees will be meeting for the first time at your event.*

Fashion Show

Spiciness: ♥
Complexity: 💣💣
Activity Level: 🔊

This one is a time-tested bridal shower game for a very good reason: it guarantees giggles, mingling, and lots of fun. Make sure you've got lots of toilet paper on hand!

Divide your shower guests into teams of three or more. The object, of course, is for each team to use one team member as a model and create a toilet paper wedding dress on her. Don't worry too much about a time limit; anyone who's finished will have a good time watching the others.

You can restrict the competition to toilet paper only or include different colors of streamers or patterned paper towels, as well. Whatever you decide, it's always good to provide scissors, glue sticks, and perhaps even needles and thread. You want your ladies to be able to maximize their artistic talents!

Once everyone is finished, it's time for the bride-to-be to choose the winning team. Award them special prizes but have edible prizes like cupcakes on hand for everyone to enjoy. They can use the dresses as napkins (but make sure you take pictures first)!

To see some of the most amazing toilet paper dresses ever, do an Internet search for "toilet paper wedding dress." These dresses are so gorgeous, they'll make you wonder why you spent so much moolah on a real dress!

Purse Pull-Out

Spiciness: up to you!
Complexity:
Activity Level:

This game exploits the inherent comedy in the sheer volume of contents in a woman's purse. You just need a list of possible purse items and some purse-toting shower guests.

Ask questions about the contents of the ladies' purses, such as:

* Who has the most pens?
* Who's got a condom?
* Who's got a tampon?
* Who has the most mirrors?
* Who's carrying photos of family members?
* Who has the most loose change at the bottom of her purse?
* Who's got a nail file?
* Who's got an unidentified key?
* Who's got a hairbrush?
* Who has a pair of underwear?
* Who has the most tubes of lip balm?
* Who has some kind of electronic item?
* Who's got a toy?
* Who has the most different flavors of gum?
* Who's got the oldest receipt?
* Who's got the item most unlikely to be found in a purse?

Whenever multiple women have an item, award the point to whoever pulls it out the quickest. Whoever has the most points at the end of the game wins! Give the winner a cute prize that will work as another addition to her purse, such as a cell phone cover, travel-sized lotion, or tiny photo album.

Memory for Marriage

Spiciness: ♥ to ♥♥♥
Complexity: 💣
Activity Level: 📢

This is a cute and easy game that will test your guests' creativity and memory. No props are needed – just some party guests with big imaginations!

The first person says, "The wedding's coming up and Heather needs...," completing the sentence with something original (and, obviously, your own bride-to-be's first name!).

The next person must repeat what the previous person said and then add her own answer. The game continues as such, getting harder with each turn.

For example, a game might go something like this:

Leah: The wedding's coming up and Heather needs a bouquet.
Rachel: The wedding's coming up and Heather needs a bouquet and a garter.
Kirsten: The wedding's coming up and Heather needs a bouquet, a garter, and wedding lingerie.
Nynne: The wedding's coming up and Heather needs a bouquet, a garter, wedding lingerie, and running shoes.
Megan: The wedding's coming up and Heather needs a bouquet, a garter, wedding lingerie, running shoes, and a manicure.
Marlene: The wedding's coming up and Heather needs a bouquet, a garter, wedding lingerie, running shoes, a manicure, and plane tickets for the honeymoon.

Keep playing until someone forgets something, then they're out. Give the last three people standing prizes.

Treasure Hunt Deluxe

Spiciness: ♥
Complexity: 🎇🎇🎇
Activity Level: 📢 📢

If you know someone with a flair for poetry, have them help you with this game. It's so much fun and it really gets people up and chatting. This one is actually quite straightforward, but it gets a high complexity rating because there is a fair amount of preparation required.

Buy a small gift for everyone coming to your shower and wrap it. Then, think of good places to hide each present at the shower location. Once you've thought up a place, come up with a short poem as a clue for the gift's location, such as:

Black and white,
Out of site,
It's played near your gift tonight!

The location? Behind the piano, of course! (If you aren't poetically inclined, feel free to write non-rhyming clues.)

Obviously, you'll have to hide everyone's gifts ahead of time. When it's time for the game, distribute everyone's clues. Then, turn them loose and let them hunt for their presents!

Here's a fun variation to keep everyone involved and working together: Give only one clue at the start and have all the guests hunt for that gift together. Have a second clue taped to the first gift so everyone can continue the hunt for the next present. Have a third clue taped to the second present, and so on. You should write one guest's name on each clue so everyone knows which present belongs to whom. Don't let anyone open their present until all of them have been found!

Candle Contest

Spiciness: ⊘
Complexity: 💣💣
Activity Level: 📢

Here is a fun, civilized game for less active, more conservative guests.

Buy several votive candles of different scents. Choose scents that are familiar to most people because this game is tougher than you might think!

Number each of the different scented candles and have your guests smell them, one by one, then write down what scent they think each one is. The person who gets the most scents correct wins the votives! If you have multiple winners, divide up the votives between them.

It's helpful to have a few small glasses filled with whole coffee beans for your guests to sniff in between candles. Coffee beans cleanse your "nose palate" so you can more easily distinguish between scents.

If you'd like, buy a special votive candleholder and one candle for the winner of this game, instead of giving them all the scented candles. Give the votives to each one of your guests as thank-you gifts. If you decide to do this, buy duplicates of the scents you used to play so you've got enough candles for everyone!

Bracelet Brain-Teaser

Check out the trivia appendix on page 169!

Spiciness: up to you!
Complexity:
Activity Level:

Here's a nice one to play if you'd like a game that's not so much an event during your bridal shower as it is a complement to the party as a whole.

This game uses those stretchy, inexpensive bracelets that you can find at dollar stores or costume jewelry shops. Choose ones that you like and buy enough so that each of your guests gets two or three.

Throughout the course of the party, trivia questions will be asked about the upcoming wedding and the soon-to-be newlyweds. Think up your own questions or borrow some from our trivia appendix on page 169.

The questions should all be written on individual pieces of paper and placed in a jar. Whenever a guest wants to try to win another bracelet, she should pull a question from the jar and read it aloud. If she can answer the question correctly, she gets to steal a bracelet from the guest of her choice. If she gets it wrong, let others try to answer. The first person who answers it correctly can steal a bracelet from the guest who asked the question in the first place.

Let everyone keep whatever bracelets they end up with. Have a special prize for the guest who wound up with the most bracelets and dub her trivia champion!

Guess the Price Raffle

Spiciness: up to you!
Complexity: ●●
Activity Level: ◀))

Here's another non-intrusive game that you can play if you don't want games to feature big in your party, but still would like to give away a prize or two. (Of course, it works just as nicely if your bridal shower is one big game-fest!)

Before the event, put together a nice gift basket with wine, cheese, crackers, grapes, nice chocolate, etc. Print out raffle tickets that have a blank for the cost of each item in the basket, as well as the total price and the guest's name. Don't forget a blank for the cost of the basket itself!

Tell your guests that whoever comes closest to guessing the total price of the basket without going over wins the basket! Leave a small box next to the basket for people to place their guesses in, along with the raffle tickets and some pencils.

You can vary this game in a lot of fun and creative ways. Could you make a gift basket to fit the theme of the bridal shower, upcoming wedding, or honeymoon? A Hawaiian honeymoon gift basket, for example, would have flip-flops, a lei, sunscreen, a pineapple, sunglasses, a beach towel, a snorkel, macadamia nuts, and the like.

You could also make multiple gift baskets: one with wine and cheese, another with bath products, and another with entertainment items (like DVDs, microwave popcorn, theatre gift certificates, etc.). They don't need to be expensive to be fun!

For sillier options, you could add "gag" gift baskets into the mix, such as one with cleaning products (complete with sponges!), one with baby items, or even one with everyday stuff like socks, underwear, flour, and eggs. There's an obvious joke here about the "romance" in the bride-to-be's future!

If you don't love the idea of people knowing what you spent on the gift baskets, do away with the price aspect of this game. Instead, have your guests examine the baskets and then try to remember their contents. Award each basket to whoever can recall the most items from that basket correctly. Settle any ties by having guests mention specific details about the items (as in: "What color are the flip-flops?" or "Where is the wine from?").

Bonus Idea: Make a gift basket with sexy items to play this game at your bachelorette party! Think g-strings, massage oil, chocolate sauce, a romance novel, and playing cards with nude men on them!

Bonus Idea: If you'd like to give away party favors, try making tiny gift baskets full of miniature candies. You can find inexpensive, cute little baskets at any craft supply store.

Other Events:

Bachelorette Party Games

Bridal showers and bachelorette parties used to be one and the same, but over the years the bachelorette party has morphed into something a little, well, dirtier.

...and thank goodness for that because lord knows a girl's got to unwind a little before she ties the knot!

Almost all of these games are designed to work just as well at home as on the go, and most include racy undertones and some form of drinking (safety plug: never drink and drive). However, that doesn't mean they won't work at more elegant bachelorette parties. All are easily modifiable to suit your crowd, plans and, most importantly, your personal tastes.

After all, this is a very special and symbolic night of serious girly time. Use these game ideas to make the most of it!

Garters

Spiciness: ♥ ♥
Complexity: 💣 💣
Activity Level: 🔊

This is a good game to play at home or anywhere else you plan on staying for awhile. It's a fabulous icebreaker because it brings out the rowdy, mildly aggressive behavior in everyone! You'll need a deck of cards (or two if you have more than six players) and enough novelty garters for everyone playing, minus one.

The object of this game is extremely simple: get four of a kind. Start by dealing four cards, face down, to every player. Put the garters in the middle of table. The dealer puts the remaining stack of cards face down to her left on the table.

To start playing, the dealer picks one card off the top of the deck and decides if she wants to keep it or not. If she doesn't, she puts it face down on her right. If she does want the card, she must exchange it for a card in her hand and discard a different card face down on her right, so she still only has four cards.

The next person then gets to look at the dealer's discards. She must do the same – pick up a card, decide whether she wants it or not, and discard the unwanted card to her right for the next player to look at. All players must only keep four cards at all times.

The last player in the circle (to the immediate left of the dealer) must throw all of her discards face up, not face down. This is so everyone in the circle can see the cards they can't have and therefore which sets of four are impossible for them to make (at least for the time being). Remember, the dealer only takes cards from the face down pile, not the face up discards. If the dealer gets through all her cards before someone gets four of a kind, she should flip the discard pile from the last player over (so that it's face down) and start going through the cards again. (Shuffling is optional.)

When one person gets four of a kind, she may take a garter. Once one garter is gone, it's a free-for-all race for the remaining garters. In other words, the rest of the players *don't* have to have four of a kind to take a garter. Whoever ends up without a garter gets the letter 'G'.

Play additional rounds to dole out more letters. You also get a letter if you've taken a garter when no one actually had four or a kind (Don't ask me why, but it happens a lot!) Whoever spells G-A-R-T-E-R is out! Keep playing until you only have winner.

You'll need to take one garter away every time someone gets eliminated, so why not punish that person by making her wear a garter for all to see? You could also make this a little racier by substituting g-strings for garters, but either way the item must be visible on the outside of the girl's clothing!

To turn this into a drinking game, make the person who gets the letter at the end of each round do a shot and/or go get refills for any ladies who have empty glasses.

Bigger and Better

Spiciness: ♥
Complexity: 💣💣
Activity Level: 📢 📢

This game is a great way to get your girls to bond. It's the perfect accompaniment to a night on the town because the ladies will have to interact with a lot of strangers in order for this game to work.

Separate the girls into teams of about four people (smaller is okay too) and give each team a safety pin. The object of the game is to trade up the safety pin for bigger and better items. When the safety pin has been traded for something else, that item should also be traded up for something better. Continue the game until a designated time, but give everyone at least a few hours.

The teams can use whatever means at their disposal to trade up their item, but there are a few rules:

* No sweetening the trades with personal items.
* All trades must be made with non-bachelorette party guests (i.e. no trading between each other).
* No money can factor into any trade.

At the end of the game, see what everyone's ended up with. You may be surprised by the results! The winner is the team with the most valuable item. Give the items to the bride as a congratulatory gift and have extra prizes ready for the winning team. You could also have prize categories, like "The Funniest," "The Worst Trade," and "The Most Expensive." It's up to you!

Mystery Drinking Game

Spiciness: ♥
Complexity: 💣💣
Activity Level: 🔊

This is a hilarious game that is guaranteed to get even drinking game haters intrigued. You don't need to play this game with alcohol, of course, and you can modify it to suit the coordination level of your guests.

The object of the game is to repeat a set pattern of body movements that involve taking sips of a drink. If a person can repeat the pattern correctly, they don't have to do a shot (or eat a handful of jelly beans or sing the alphabet song or whatever you decide on). If they can't repeat it correctly, they have to do the "punishment" and it's the next person's turn.

Here's an example of a pattern:

1. Scratch your forehead with your left hand.
2. Pick up your glass with your right hand, set it down.
3. Pick up your glass with your left hand, tap it once on the table, take a drink, set it down.
4. Pick up your glass with your right hand, tap it twice on the table, take two sips, set it down.
5. Pick up your glass with your left hand, tap it three times on the table, pass it to your right hand, take three sips, set it down.
6. Pick up your glass with your right hand, set it down.
7. Rest both hands on the table.

Whoever leads this game has to memorize the pattern so they can perform it fairly automatically. It doesn't need to be quick, but it does need to flow. The idea is to trick people into thinking they've got the pattern memorized so they're willing to risk trying it out. Usually people will forget the minor variations in the pattern or leave out the first or last step because they don't realize it's part of the pattern (yet).

Whenever someone goofs up, *do not* tell them what they did wrong – just inflict their punishment and move on to the next person. Don't worry – everyone figures it out eventually... usually. (Tee hee!)

Bonus Idea*: Have wine glasses or beer mugs engraved with your guests' names so they can play this game using their own personalized glasses and then take them home as souvenirs.*

Bachelorette Souvenirs

Spiciness: ♥ ♥
Complexity: 💣 💣
Activity Level: 📢 📢

Here's a little competition for your bachelorette party guests. This game only works for parties away from home.

Before you go out, make a list of items that need to be collected over the course of the evening and give each girl a copy, as well as a small gift bag in which to keep her finds.

Here are some items you could come across:

* ✳ bar coasters
* ✳ a matchbook
* ✳ a drink umbrella
* ✳ a man's phone number
* ✳ a foreigner's business card
* ✳ a feather
* ✳ some fast food packaging
* ✳ a flavored or colored condom
* ✳ a bathroom graffiti quote
* ✳ a cherry stem with a knot in it

You should also think up some items that are specific to the place(s) you're going to. Try to have at least 15 items on the list.

Have a prize ready for whoever collects all the items on her list first. Give her a bottle of wine, some sexy undies, or the like. For the losers, tell them they can keep those men's phone numbers as prizes!

Bachelorette Scavenger Hunt

Make photocopies of page 193!

Spiciness: ♥ ♥ ♥
Complexity: 💣 💣
Activity Level: 📢 📢

This game is like *Bachelorette Souvenirs* except it's about a bajillion times racier. Play this one with your most adventurous girlfriends.

Instead of competing, your ladies will be working together to check items off the scavenger hunt list. Make sure you've got at least one digital camera available for photographic evidence of the action!

For the complete reproducible list, see page 193. For now, here are a few ideas to get your juices flowing:

* Dance with a stripper
* Get a man's boxer shorts
* Ask a blond for their phone number
* Photograph a urinal
* Kiss a strange woman
* Kiss a strange man
* Have a man serenade the bride
* Get a man to buy someone a drink
* Buy something icky from an "Adults Only" store

If you'd like, have consequences for this game. Make everyone do a shot for every unchecked "to do," for example.

For any items that don't produce physical evidence (like someone serenading the bride), photos are required. Be sure to have the photos printed and put in an album for a reminder of your crazy night!

Queens and Wenches

Spiciness: ♥
Complexity: 💣💣
Activity Level: 📢📢

There is something about this game that just gets funnier the more the drinks are flowing. You can definitely play it without alcohol, but make sure you've got a video camera ready if you do!

Have enough seating for all the ladies. Arrange the chairs in a semi-circle so that everyone can see each other. One end of the semi-circle will be the "Queen" seat and the other end will be the "Wench" seat. The in-between seats will be various ranks. You may want to put signs on the back of each chair in case you forget the order at some point in the evening!

Here is the typical order of ranks/seats:

1. Queen
2. Princess
3. Duchess
4. Countess
5. Baroness
6. Lady in Waiting
7. Courtier
8. Commoner
9. Wench

To play, have everyone sit down in a seat randomly, except for the bride-to-be, who should start in the "Queen" seat. Once everyone is seated, tell them their ranks and then explain the rules.

The Queen starts by calling out a rank other than her own. The person who is currently sitting in that rank must immediately call out the name of another rank, also not her own.

The idea is not to skip a beat. If someone causes any delay when it's their turn, they're demoted to the "Wench" seat and the ladies who were lower ranked than she was all get to move up a spot.

Raise the hilarity factor by making the new Wench take a shot or do something embarrassing (à la "truth or dare"). If the game starts to get too easy, let the Queen make up new rules, such as:

* You can no longer call out the rank of the person who just called you.
* You can only call ranks below your own, except for the Wench, who can call any rank.
* The Duchess has to say, "Good luck, my Queen!" before every round or she is automatically demoted to "Wench."

If you have fewer than nine guests, feel free to delete some ranks. If you have a lot of guests, it's perfectly okay to have repeats of any of the above ranks, except for "Queen" and "Wench."

If you're willing to get a touch more complicated, play a hit variation of this game by using one or two decks of cards and the rules to the card game called "President." Basically, you deal out all the cards and the object is to get rid of everything in your hand by laying multiples of the same card (don't worry about suits). Whoever goes out first is the Queen; the last one to go out is the Wench.

For the full rules to this game (plus a bunch of ideas for crazy things the Queen can make her subjects do), do an Internet search for "President card game."

Oh no, I Never!

Make photocopies of pages 194-198!

Spiciness: ♥♥♥
Complexity: 💣
Activity Level: 🔊

If you thought you knew everything about your girlfriends, get ready to learn a whole lot more. *Oh no, I Never!* is a spicy little game that is guaranteed to get the girls talking.

Ahead of time, prepare a couple of dozen cards with statements that start with "I've never..." Some ideas are:

* I've never made out in an elevator.
* I've never stuffed my bra.
* I've never lied about my age.
* I've never had sex in a public place.
* I've never gone skinny-dipping.
* I've never stolen anything.
* I've never gone into a men's washroom.
* I've never sunbathed in the nude.
* I've never used a sex toy.

See our complete set of photocopiable *Oh no, I Never!* cards on pages 194-198.

To play, simply have one guest choose a card and read the statement aloud. If anyone disagrees with the statement (i.e. they *have* done it before), they must be punished! Make them do a shot and/or recount the juicy details of their illicit activities.

Smokin' Hot Potato

Spiciness: ♥ ♥ ♥
Complexity: 💣
Activity Level: 🔊

Everyone knows how to play hot potato. Here's a feisty version to encourage some girlish giggling and maybe even a little bit of blushing!

For this game, play some spicy music like "You Sexy Thing," "Ladies' Night," or "Strokin'." The item is passed around your circle of ladies while the music is playing. When the music stops, the lady holding the item is out.

The item in question should be something at least R-rated, such as a vibrator, a DVD of a male strip show, or a set of racy lingerie. The last lady remaining in the game gets the prize!

For a fun variation, fill a basket with enough sexy gifts for every lady at your party. Pass the basket and, when the music stops, let the lucky lady holding the basket select the item of her choice. Keep playing until everyone's got a gift.

If you're on a budget, you could choose affordable items like g-strings, massage oil, or mugs with muscled, half-naked men on the side. Visit a novelty shop for tacky - but hilarious - inspiration.

Bachelorette Bingo

Make photocopies of pages 199-202!

Spiciness: ♥♥♥
Complexity: 💣
Activity Level: 🔊

This game is great because it keeps the girls in party mode throughout the whole night. All you need are the game cards (make your own or use ours on pages 199-202) and some pencils.

At the start of the evening, distribute the cards and pencils to all the guests except the bride-to-be. The object of this game is simple: cross off as many words on your card as possible. Anytime the bride-to-be says a word on your card, you can cross it off. You can't tell her to say a certain word and you can't overtly try to make her guess which words are on your card. The words should just come out as a result of "natural" conversation.

Many of the words, like "wedding," "bachelorette," and "mother-in-law," will come out fairly naturally. The game gets funny when the girls try to steer the conversation in bizarre directions that will lead the bride to say a word like "penis" or "porno." Award a prize to whoever finishes their card first or whoever has the most words crossed off by the end of the evening.

You may want to make your own cards so the game is more personalized (for example, with people's names, cities, etc.). If you do this, make sure all the cards are different so everyone doesn't win at the same time!

Sexy Word Sleuth

Spiciness: ♥♥♥
Complexity: 💣💣
Activity Level: 🔊

Here's a fun one to play if your bachelorette party is staying in one place, at least for awhile. For this game, you can either make a bunch of square cards with individual letters on them or purchase a Scrabble game so the work's already done for you.

To play, give every player eight letters. The object is to try to make a word of at least three letters that has "sexy" undertones. Each word must be accompanied by a short explanation of why the word is sexy. It does not need to be an overtly sexual word or even an actual dictionary word, as long as the speller has an explanation for how her word relates to sex. (This makes the game extra interesting as people explain how "tie" or "jelly" count as sexy words.)

The first person to form a word out of three or more of her letters places the word down on the playing surface and draws enough cards to replenish her stock. Then it's the next person's turn. Each subsequent word must use at least one letter from a word that's already been played, so the words overlap (like a crossword puzzle).

When someone is unable to play or when the group deems her word "un-sexy," she should be subjected to a punishment of some sort – take a drink, reveal a secret, or do a dare of the group's choosing. Once she's completed her punishment, she has the option of swapping out half of her letters for new ones.

Keep playing until all your letters are used up or no more words can be formed. If you'd like, give out prizes for the most subversively sexy word, the most obviously sexy word, the funniest word, the dirtiest word, the longest word, etc.

Big Night Out

Make photocopies of pages 203-205!

Spiciness: up to you!
Complexity:
Activity Level:

Celebrate the bride's final days of singledom in style with *Big Night Out*, the game that helps you paint the town red!

Come up with some fabulous ideas for bachelorette party events. Put each idea on a strip of paper and seal them in individual envelopes. Put all the sealed envelopes in a gift bag, along with a pair of dice, and get ready to have a night of spontaneous fun!

Start by opening the first envelope. Everyone must then do whatever is on the paper. Remember to bring the gift bag with the envelopes with you, because you'll need those to carry on with the festivities!

Here are some ideas for games and events:

* Go to the strip club. The first girl to put a dollar in a dancer's g-string chooses the next envelope!

* Get manicures. The girl whose nails dry first opens the next envelope.

* Go to the nearest pub. Everyone must order a drink. Get out the dice and take turns rolling. If you roll anything with a six or adding up to six, you don't have to drink. If you roll snake eyes (two ones), you must do a shot. Any other roll is one big sip of your drink! The person who finishes her drink first gets to open the next envelope.

* Visit an "Adults Only" store. Whoever finds the grossest item opens the next envelope.

* Go to a casino and play the slots with five dollars each. The lady who wins the most (or takes the most time to lose) gets to choose the next envelope.

* Go to a nightclub and get as many hunky men as possible to dance with the bride-to-be. Let her choose the next envelope!

* Visit a karaoke bar. The first girl(s) to get up and sing can choose shots for the rest of the ladies to do. The last person to sing gets to open the next envelope.

* All ladies must go to the restroom in a nightclub and put all their underwear on over top of their clothing. Start dancing! The first person to get a comment on their apparel opens the next envelope.

It doesn't matter if you don't get through all the envelopes in the evening, but you can make it your mission if you want to! The idea is to have as much fun as possible, so make the night your own!

If you like the ideas above, feel free to use the complete set of reproducible cards on pages 203-205. You'll also find some blank cards so you can add your own ideas into the mix.

Remember, if you plan on doing anything that involves alcohol, consider renting a limo for the evening or have a designated driver. There's also the good old-fashioned taxi and/or subway!

Other Events:

Sunday Brunch/ Gift-Opening Day Games

Don't kid yourself: as exciting as that pile of gifts is, not everyone will love sitting there watching the happy couple unwrap their loot all day long.

Games are the ideal way to entertain your guests and make your Sunday brunch and/or gift-opening a lot more enjoyable, but they shouldn't drag on too long or you'll never get through your stack.

These games work well on their own if you're taking a longer break, waiting for everyone to arrive, or even eating, but you can also play any one of them in two minutes or less - perfect for a small, super-charged dose of entertainment in between presents.

Secret Code

Spiciness: ♥
Complexity: 💣
Activity Level: 📢

This is a super easy game for your event because it can be played throughout the gift opening, a meal, or even during other games! All you need are some sheets of stickers and a secret word.

The word you choose should be something fairly common that people will say quite a bit, such as "good," "nice," or "present." Don't choose something too generic (like "the") or you'll run out of stickers before the game is over!

Keep the chosen word a secret from your guests, but do tell them that anyone who says the secret word will receive a sticker. Whoever can figure out what the secret word is will get a prize.

Slap a sticker on anyone who says your secret word, but don't do it immediately after it comes out of people's mouths. The idea is for them to be wondering what they just said, so make sure they utter at least a few more words before you give them their sticker.

Have a gift ready for whoever correctly guesses your secret word. For extra chuckles, award a second prize to the person who managed to collect the most stickers without figuring out what the secret word was!

Wedding Buzzword

Make photocopies of pages 206-211!

Spiciness: ♥
Complexity: 💣💣💣
Activity Level: 🔊

Wedding Buzzword is a great way to get guests at your brunch or gift-opening mingling and enjoying the day. This game gets a high complexity rating because of the preparation required ahead of time and the fact that you'll have to explain the rules to the guests, but don't be daunted – it's worth the effort. (I mean it – it's so so so SO fun!)

Start by preparing a good number – 50 or more – of wedding-related words or phrases and print them out on index cards (or just use ours on pages 206-211). You'll want to use words like:

* Nuptials
* Bouquet
* Buffet dinner
* Pop the question
* The Wedding March
* Pipe organ
* Wedding planner
* White Wedding
* Caterer
* Cocktails

* Boutonnieres
* Something old, something new, something borrowed, something blue
* Here Comes the Bride
* Wedding gown
* Flower petals
* For richer, for poorer
* Ring bearer

You'll also need a stopwatch (or steal one of those little hourglasses from a board game). Each round lasts two minutes. To play, everyone must sit in a circle and number off 1,2,1,2,1,2... so that every other person is on the same team (either team 1 or team 2). You could also have people "number" off into "Team Bride" and "Team Groom."

The first person pulls one of the index cards from a hat and has to try to make his teammates say the word on the card. He can't say any of the word(s) on the card and he can't point at anything in the room.

Once the word has been guessed, the hat is passed to the next person (who is on the opposite team). Now it's that person's turn to pull a card and try to guess it. If the team can't guess the word, too bad! They just have to keep trying until the time runs out. When that happens, the team that is *not* holding the hat gets a point.

If you want to play more than just a round at a time, keep playing up to a predetermined number of points. Ten is a good number, but don't be surprised when the guests want a rematch!

If you have a lot of guests at your event, consider having two or more *Wedding Buzzword* circles on the go so people don't have to wait for eons to get a turn.

Bonus Idea: If your brunch is of the more formal variety, consider using the game cards as place cards at the tables.

Bonus Idea: Create a few of your own personalized game cards. Use the names of people close to the bride and groom or of pertinent places, such as where the couple got engaged or where the honeymoon will be.

Don't Say It!

Make photocopies of pages 212-217!

Spiciness: ♥
Complexity: 💣💣💣
Activity Level: 📢

Like the previous game, *Don't Say It!* requires a fair bit of advanced preparation, but is well worth it. You'll be rewarded with a great party game that gets your guests laughing, interacting, and talking about how your wedding was the best one ever!

For this game, you'll also need some kind of timer as well as pre-prepared game cards. These cards should have a wedding word or phrase on them along with four or five words that you can't say when you're trying to make your teammates guess what's on the card.

For example, let's say your card looks like this:

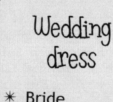

Wedding dress

* Bride
* Gown
* Wears
* Clothing

(Make your own cards or use ours on pages 212-217.)

You've got to make the other people on your team say "Wedding Dress" by explaining it without saying the words "wedding," "dress," "bride," "gown," "wears," or "clothing." You also can't say any variation of the above words (e.g. "wear," "clothes," and "dresses" are out).

To get the game going, divide your guests into four teams. If you've got an especially large group of people, have two games going rather than adding extra teams. This way people won't have to wait too long to play.

The first team starts by pulling a game card from a hat. They have a designated amount of time for their turn, usually a minute. Once the team has guessed what's on the card, a different team member from the same team pulls another card and the team continues. When the time runs out, the team gets a point for each card that they correctly guessed. Then it's the next team's turn.

You can play this game up to a certain number of points or for a certain number of turns. Either way, your guests will have barrels of fun with *Don't Say It!*

Bonus Idea: When it's time to write thank-you notes, use the back of the game cards in place of normal stationery. Your guests will appreciate the reminder of the fun they had at your event.

W-E-D-D-I-N-G P-R-E-S-E-N-T-S

Spiciness: ♥
Complexity: 💣
Activity Level: 📣

This is another simple game that can be played throughout the course of your event with minimal intrusion. All you need are some blank sheets of paper, as well as some pencils for your guests.

The object of this game is to think up as many words as possible using only the letters in the phrase "Wedding Presents." All words must be at least three letters long and you cannot duplicate letters (e.g. you can use only one 'w' and a maximum of three 'e's because that's how many are in the phrase).

Just for fun, here are a dozen awesome (wedding-themed, no less!) words hiding in "Wedding Presents":

✳ Witness	✳ Wine	✳ Dinner
✳ Singer	✳ Weeps	✳ Dessert
✳ Tender	✳ Dress	✳ Entwined
✳ Pews	✳ Rings	✳ Tenderness

Let guests play at their leisure. At a set time, ask your guests who's got the longest list. They're the winner! You could also give bonus prizes for the longest word, the most "weddingy" word, the funniest word, etc.

Alternatively, consider personalizing this game by using the names of the newlyweds instead of "Wedding Presents." Use an online word un-scrambler to see which of your ideas are viable options (you might not be able to find too many words if the couple's names are Kirbi and Drew). Just do an Internet search for "word unscrambler" to find a list of websites that can help you out.

Gambling for Gifts

Spiciness: ♥
Complexity: 💣💣
Activity Level: 🔊

Why should the newlyweds be the only ones to get stuff? For this game, you'll need more dollar store gifts (wrapped) than you have guests and a pair of dice.

Seat everyone around a table and put all the gifts in the middle. It's great if the gifts have unusual shapes or make curious sounds. Your guests are going to be vying for them without knowing what they are!

First, set a timer for 15 minutes. Then, the first person rolls the dice. If they get a six on either die or a total of six on both (like a two and a four), they get to choose a present from the middle, but they can't unwrap it. Then they pass the dice on to the next person. If they don't get a six, they just pass on the dice without taking a present.

Make sure you've got at least one gift per person on the table, but don't worry if one player amasses a half dozen presents and someone else has none. There will be plenty of chances to equal it out!

Once all the gifts are gone from the middle, keep taking turns rolling the dice, but now when people get a six, they can steal presents from other players. Remember, everything is still wrapped!

When the timer goes off, it's time for everyone to unwrap their presents. Won't they be surprised when that pretty wrapped box they wanted so badly was just a carton of bran flakes!

When everyone is finished opening, give people five minutes to trade with one another. It's always fun to bargain your way up the gift ladder!

Fast-Paced Foreheads

Make photocopies of pages 218-221!

Spiciness: ♥
Complexity: 💣
Activity Level: 📢

Here's a quick game that can be played when coffee is being served, the groom is on the phone, or while the bride takes a bathroom break.

Have a stack of game cards ready with the name of a place on each one. Examples are the Eiffel Tower, Brazil, the Roman Coliseum, New York City... make up your own or just use our reproducible cards on pages 218-221. Either way, make sure you've got a lot of cards on hand!

When you want to play a round, choose one lucky guest and give them a game card. Tell them they must hold it up to their forehead without looking at it. The object of the game is for the guest to guess the name of the place on their forehead by only asking 'yes' or 'no' questions, such as:

* Is it in Europe?
* Is it as tall as a skyscraper?
* Is it made of stone?
* Is it a city?

Once they've guessed, give another guest a turn. Raise the fun factor by trying to get through as many people as you can during any given break time.

Gym Sock Guessing Game

Spiciness: ♥ ♥
Complexity: 💣 💣
Activity Level: 📣

Now that the wedding's over, everyone's going to be talking about the honeymoon. Here's a quirky game that will get them started while simultaneously testing the sensitivity of their feet!

Before the event, buy several pairs of gym socks (black tube socks work best) and inside each one, place an item that relates to the bride and groom's upcoming honeymoon. Here are some examples:

- ✳ sunscreen
- ✳ swim goggles
- ✳ condoms
- ✳ flip-flops
- ✳ aspirin

- ✳ camera
- ✳ sunglasses (use cheap ones!)
- ✳ a Speedo
- ✳ a little bottle of alcohol
- ✳ a 'do not disturb' doorknob sign

The items should not be visible at all from the outside.

When it's time for the game, choose some players (or if you've got a small group, have enough socks for everyone). Give the players a sock each and tell them they've got to figure out what's inside by using only their feet. They can put their feet inside the sock or just probe from the outside, but no hands allowed! Remember to give them a hint: all items are somehow related to the upcoming honeymoon.

Give the contents of the socks away as prizes, or save them for the bride and groom and award the gym socks to the winning guests!

To make this game more elegant, do away with the gym socks and just wrap the items. Players can still use their feet to guess what's in the packages, if you'd like, or let them use their hands - it's up to you!

Domestic Investigation

Check out the trivia appendix on page 169!

Spiciness: ♥ ♥
Complexity: 💣
Activity Level: 📢

Here's another trivia game that's designed to be played in short bursts when either the bride or the groom goes out of earshot. You'll need some small, sweet treats to give the newlyweds - chocolate kisses are perfect.

Have a series of questions ready about domestic life, such as:

* Who does the dishes more often?
* What's the bride's/groom's biggest pet peeve about their mate's household habits?
* Which way does he/she prefer to have the toilet paper roll?
* Has the bride/groom ever ruined an article of clothing belonging to their mate? If yes, what was it?
* What is the next big purchase the newlyweds are saving up for?

Come up with more ideas on your own or steal a few from our trivia appendix on page 169.

Whenever one of the newlyweds leaves to refill a drink or visit the bathroom, quickly ask the other one a trivia question from your list. When the person returns, re-ask the question to that person. If their answers match, they each get a chocolate kiss!

Add another dimension to this game by having consequences prepared whenever the bride or groom gets an answer wrong. Maybe they have to drink a full glass of water, tickle each other for 15 seconds, or do their best imitation of a bad first kiss.

Danger Mime!

Make photocopies of pages 222-225!

Spiciness: ♥♥
Complexity: 💣💣
Activity Level: 📢 📢

Here's a charades-type game that will definitely get people smiling as they imagine all the slapstick chaos that could happen in the newly-weds' home!

Have a series of cards ready for people to mime. The actions on the cards should all be dangerous things that could happen in or around the newlyweds' home. Here are a few of our ideas:

* A frying pan is left unattended.
* Too many plugs in the socket!
* A spill is not cleaned up.
* No spare key for the house!
* No one takes the trash out for a month. (Death by flies!)
* The cable bill doesn't get paid. (Death by boredom!)
* Rollerblades left on the staircase!

(See our complete list on ready-to-go photocopiable cards on pages 222-225.)

When you're ready to play a round, ask for a volunteer to be the "Danger Mime." The first person to correctly guess the predicament that the Danger Mime has found himself in this time gets a point. Whoever has the most points at the end of the festivities wins a prize!

Bonus Idea: *Award a prize to the mime who fakes the best death scene during his dangerous situation. After all, don't people love watching mimes suffer?*

The Best Advice for a Happy Life

Spiciness: ♥ to ♥♥♥
Complexity: 💣💣
Activity Level: 📣

This is a great game for your brunch and/or gift opening because your guests can participate at their leisure. It will be a nice diversion for whenever they want to get up and stretch their legs or take a break from watching the couple open presents.

Set up several "advice areas" around the room. At each one, put blank recipe cards and a few pens. It's nice to use different colored cards for each station, or have them custom-made to suit your party theme. Have a pretty box ready to store your cards as a souvenir from the day.

Tell your guests to share their wisdom on marriage's biggest questions whenever they've got inspiration. Each area will be assigned a different type of advice - put up signs so they know which one they're at. You may also want to remind your guests once or twice throughout the gathering to go write their thoughts down, if you feel your advice-o-meter is a little low!

Here are some potential questions for your "advice areas":

* How can the bride and groom have fun on a budget?
* How do you know when you've had enough kids?
* How should the chores be divided?
* What are some tips for making a little extra cash when money's tight?
* How should political disputes be settled?

It's good for the questions to range from strange to silly to sincere. You'll get a good blend of funny and practical advice that may actually get used from time to time!

Bonus Section:

Trivia Appendix

If you plan on playing games at your wedding (which I assume is what you're reading this for!), you'll find that many excellent games, including several in this book, make use of trivia questions about the newly-weds, their wedding, and weddings in general.

Trivia works well in all kinds of game scenarios, but often the hardest part for game planners is actually coming up with the questions.

Never fear - it's the trivia appendix to the rescue!

This section contains 175 of questions to inspire you (or copy outright!). Use them in our games or as inspiration for speeches and/or icebreakers.

Congratulations - game planning just got way easier!

Trivia Questions

* What flowers are in the bride's bouquet?
* Who did a reading/sang a song at the ceremony?
* What countries were represented by the guests at the ceremony?
* What did the pew decorations look like at the ceremony?
* What time did the ceremony actually start?
* What color are the bridesmaids' dresses?

* What kind of fabric is the wedding gown made of?
* Name five people sitting in the front row at the ceremony.
* How many ushers were there at the ceremony?
* What was on the cover of the ceremony programs?
* Who said their vows first, the bride or the groom?
* What flowers were in the groomsmen's boutonnieres?

* What music was playing while the bride was walking down the aisle?
* What was the weather like the day the couple got their marriage license?
* Did the couple go ring shopping together before the engagement?
* What day did they get engaged?
* What was the groom wearing when the couple got engaged?
* What is the bride's/groom's favorite food?

* When was the last time the groom gave the bride flowers?
* Where did the bride and groom meet?
* What is the bride's/groom's middle name?
* Where did the couple get engaged?
* How many people are/were at the wedding?

* What anniversary are the bride's/groom's parents celebrating this year?
* How many pets does the couple have/want?
* Who is taller - the bride or groom? By how much?
* Where will the couple live?
* Where did the groom get the engagement ring?

* What is the bride's favorite sport?
* Where did the bride/groom go to high school?
* How many times did the bride try on her wedding dress (counting the wedding day)?
* What was the bride wearing on the couple's first date?
* Which does the bride/groom prefer: the toilet paper rolling off the top or off the bottom?

* Where will the couple go on their honeymoon?
* How long is their honeymoon for?
* Where did the bride meet her maid of honor?
* How long has the groom known his best man?
* What does the bride/groom eat when he/she has a midnight craving?

* What country does the bride/groom most want to travel to?
* Who steals the blankets - bride or groom?
* Who's going to do the most diaper changing?
* Who would win a snoring contest?
* Who will go gray first?

* Who's the better dancer?
* Who's more afraid of sharks/spiders/bears?
* Who's most likely to burn boiling water?
* Who will be first to notice dirty socks that don't make it to the hamper?
* Who's more addicted to coffee/cola/iced tea?

* Who will be most likely to join a lawn bowling league?
* Who likes horror movies more?
* Who is more likely to put a red sock in the white laundry load?
* Who will be first to forget a birthday/anniversary?
* Who will be first to cry at their children's graduation?

* Who wanted to get married first?
* Who will be the first to give up learning about new-fangled technology?
* Who has traveled to the most countries?
* Who is more likely to end up on a reality TV show?
* Who is secretly planning their pop music debut?

* Who will help the kids with their homework more often?
* Who will be the first to say, "Kids, you're old enough to make your own lunches!"?
* Who is more likely to say, "No (more) pets!"?
* Who has to get up more to go to the bathroom in the middle of the night?
* Who likes dessert more?

* Who is more likely to develop a weird phobia - bride or groom?
* Who still listens to their favorite bands from middle school?
* Who likes fruity, "girly" drinks more?
* Who loses their keys/cell phone/TV remote more often?
* Who would probably volunteer for the PTA?

* Who will be the first to suggest new bedroom techniques?
* Who's the bigger pack rat?
* Who had more secret house parties without telling their parents?
* Who thinks off-color jokes are funnier?
* Who is more of a dog person/cat person?

✳ Who is more afraid of the dentist?
✳ Who is more adventurous with foreign food?
✳ Who is more of a social butterfly?
✳ Who is more likely to make it into the *Guinness Book of World Records*?
✳ When is the mother-in-law's birthday?
✳ Would the couple's dream house be in the city or the country?

✳ What was a honeymoon option the couple did not end up choosing?
✳ How old were the bride and groom when they first met?
✳ When the bride was younger, at what age did she expect to get married?
✳ How long has the couple been together?
✳ Where did the bride/groom grow up?

✳ What flavor of cake does the bride like best?
✳ Does the bride/groom prefer red or white wine?
✳ Did the bride/groom ever have an imaginary friend?
✳ What did the bride/groom want to be when he/she grew up?
✳ Did the couple live together before they got engaged/married? How long?

✳ Which guest traveled the furthest to come to the wedding?
✳ Which relative was first to meet their future daughter-in-law/son-in-law?
✳ On which leg is the bride wearing her garter?
✳ Whose little black book was bigger before the happy couple got together?
✳ Did the groom ever make the bride a mixed tape/CD?

✳ Where did the couple go on their first date?
✳ What's the craziest hair color the bride/groom has ever had?
✳ How old was the bride/groom when she/he had her/his first kiss?
✳ Where did the bride and groom share their first kiss?
✳ What kind of car will the groom want when he has his midlife crisis?

✳ Who is the bride's/groom's least favorite singer?
✳ Which drawer are the groom's socks in?
✳ How many times was the bride a bridesmaid before she got married?
✳ Does the couple make their bed every morning? Who makes it more often?
✳ How many aunts and uncles does the bride/groom have?

✳ How many cousins does the couple have in total?
✳ What is the bride's/groom's biggest pet peeve about his/her mate?
✳ If the bride/groom could retire to anywhere, where would it be?
✳ What time of day was the bride/groom born?
✳ Did the groom get down on one knee when he proposed?

✳ What is the bride's/groom's least favorite chore?
✳ Did the groom ask the bride's parents' permission to marry their daughter?
✳ What color car does the bride/groom/couple have?
✳ What color car would the bride/groom/couple like to have?
✳ Which is the bride's/groom's least favorite sport?

* What was the maid of honor's/best man's first impression of the bride/groom?
* Which famous person would the bride/groom have most wanted to marry?
* Which is the bride's/groom's favorite cartoon?
* Which is the bride's/groom's favorite flavor of ice cream?
* Which is the bride's/groom's favorite fast food restaurant?

* What was the bride's/groom's worst ever violation of the law?
* What was the first movie the couple saw together?
* What is the bride's/groom's current favorite band?
* Where did the parents first meet their future daughter-in-law/son-in-law?
* What countries/states has the couple traveled to together?
* What year did the bride/groom graduate?

* What is the bride's "something blue"?
* What flavor is the wedding cake?
* How many people assisted at the ceremony, including ushers, officiants, musicians, bridal party, etc.?
* What is the bride and groom's official "our song?"
* What is the bride's/groom's favorite sports team?

* How many bones has the bride/groom broken in her/his lifetime?
* Has the bride/groom ever had braces?
* What is the bride's/groom's favorite movie?
* Is the bride/groom baptized?
* Where is the weirdest place the newlyweds ever went on a date?

* Which does the bride prefer: soap operas or sitcoms?
* Which does the groom prefer: beer or mixed drinks?
* Which does the bride/groom prefer: crossword puzzles or card games?
* Which does the bride/groom prefer: foot massages or a favorite meal?
* Which does the bride/groom prefer: museums or musicals?

* Where did the bride's/groom's parents get married?
* What is the couple's wedding website's URL (web address)?
* What kind of dressing was on the salad at dinner?
* Who tried the wedding cake first after the cake cutting?
* What was the date of the bachelorette party/bachelor party?

* Who plays Muriel in *Muriel's Wedding*? (Answer: Toni Collette)
* Which composer's "Canon in D" is a wedding ceremony favorite? (Answer: Johann Pachelbel)
* Who gets left at the altar in *The Wedding Singer*? (Answer: actor Adam Sandler playing Robbie Hart)
* In Nat King Cole's song "L-O-V-E," what does 'V' stand for? (Answer: "very very extraordinary")
* Who was the conniving best friend in *My Best Friend's Wedding*? (Answer: Julia Roberts)

* Name three Beatles songs with the word "love" in them. (Possible answers: "Yesterday," "And I Love Her," "I Will," "Michelle," "She Loves You" ...)
* What is the wife of a Marquis called? (Answer: a Marquess or Marchioness)
* How does Jennifer Lopez meet her dream man in *The Wedding Planner*? (Answer: She is planning his wedding!)
* In *Gone With the Wind*, who told Scarlett that she "should be kissed and often, and by someone who knows how?" (Answer: Rhett Butler)
* Name five wedding-themed movies. (Possible answers: *Four Weddings and a Funeral, Meet the Fockers, Betsy's Wedding, Runaway Bride, Much Ado About Nothing, Mama Mia!, Made of Honor, Monsoon Wedding...*)

* Which actresses play feuding best friends in the film *Bride Wars*? (Answer: Kate Hudson and Anne Hathaway)
* Which composer penned the famous "Wedding March?" (Answer: Felix Mendelssohn)
* What is the actual title of the classic wedding processional "Here Comes the Bride?" (Answer: "Bridal Chorus")
* What actor plays anxious dad George Banks in the film *Father of the Bride*? (Answer: Steve Martin)
* In the original 1950 movie *Father of the Bride*, who plays the blushing bride-to-be? (Answer: Elizabeth Taylor)

* Who originally sang the song "I Will Always Love You," covered in 1992 by Whitney Houston for the film *The Bodyguard*? (Answer: Dolly Parton)
* How many times has Tom Cruise been married? (Answer: three)
* Who sings the wedding classic "Chapel of Love?" (Answer: The Dixie Cups)
* Who sings the song "Then He Kissed Me?" (Answer: The Crystals)
* What is the profession of the groom-to-be's mother in *Meet the Fockers*? (Answer: sex therapist)

* In what movie do actors Vince Vaughn and Owen Wilson pose as wedding guests to meet women? (Answer: *Wedding Crashers*)
* Name three types of wedding gown trains. (Possible answers: chapel length, sweeping, royal, cathedral...)
* Name three bridal magazines. (Possible answer: The Knot, Brides, Modern Bride, Bridal Guide, Martha Stewart Weddings...)
* What is the name of the princess in *The Princess Bride*? (Answer: Buttercup)
* What does the bride's father use as a cure-all in the movie *My Big Fat Greek Wedding*? (Answer: Windex)

* Who sings "Today I Met the Boy I'm Gonna Marry?" (Answer: Darlene Love)
* In what movie is a young single woman dismayed at having been a bridesmaid 27 times? (Answer: *27 Dresses*)
* What is the average number of bridesmaids in an American wedding party? (Answer: four)
* What percentage of brides receive a diamond engagement ring? (Answer: 74%)
* What is the traditional dress color for Chinese brides? (Answer: red)

Bonus Section:

Photocopiable Pages

This section contains photocopiable pages for many of the games in this book.

Feel free to use them for inspiration or just photo-copy them to make your game planning that much easier!

For each photocopiable element, you'll find refer-ences back to the actual game in the book as well as any specific instructions necessary for the photocop-ies themselves.

Have fun and happy photocopying - just don't get busted using up all the toner at work!

Game instructions are on page 23. Personalize this game by including a photo of the bride and groom in the background or making your own customized word scrambles!

(Answers: wedding ring, honeymoon, kissing, proposal, wedding gown, flowers, groomsman, party, dance, presents, ceremony, tuxedo, marriage, bachelor, invitations, love, couple, fairy tale)

Wedding Scramble

See if you can unscramble the mixed-up wedding words below!

wingedd grin _____●

oh no money _____●

skiings _____●

o poplars _____●

eww dingdong _____●

wolfers _____●

monograms _____●

pry at _____●

acned _____●

serpents _____●

my encore _____●

ox duet _____●

armi rage _____●

be choral _____●

visitationn _____●

vole _____●

clue op _____●

eat fraily _____●

Marriage for Dummies

These are recipe-card sized photocopiable rectangles
to use in the game on page 24.

My best marriage advice is...

ABG

From: _____●

My best marriage advice is...

ABG

From: _____●

Bingo Bliss

Game instructions are on page 42. Personalize this game by including funny pictures of the bride and groom's faces in the squares!

Remember, all cards must be different or you could wind up with 150 winners.

Photocopy then cut out the squares on page 181. To make bingo cards, place the squares randomly on the bingo card templates (page 180) using removable sticky tack and photocopy. Alternatively, just make enough copies of the blank bingo card templates and have your guests think up their own wedding-related items and draw/write them on their cards themselves. Remember to supply the pencils!

Either way, photocopy and cut out the squares on page 181 to use as game cards for the game host. Also, feel free to enlarge both the card templates and the game cards if you feel that they are too small.

Bingo Bliss

Bingo Bliss

Bingo Bliss

Love Limericks

Compose your very own Love Limerick for the newlyweds!

ABC

Composed by:

See original game instructions on page 52. (White this part out before photocopying!)

www.TheAlternativeBride.com

Coloring Contest

Game instructions are on page 63.
Personalize this game by including black
and white caricatures of the bride and
groom for your guests to color!

Pages 184-186 are photocopiable coloring pages
for you to use in this game. Page 187, which is
mostly blank, has been included in case you'd
like your guests to draw their best impression
of the bride and groom, rather than color.

Don't forget to save your favorites for
the wedding scrapbook!

Name:_____ Table:_____

www.TheAlternativeBride.com

Name:_____ Table:_____

Name:_____ Table:_____

www.TheAlternativeBride.com

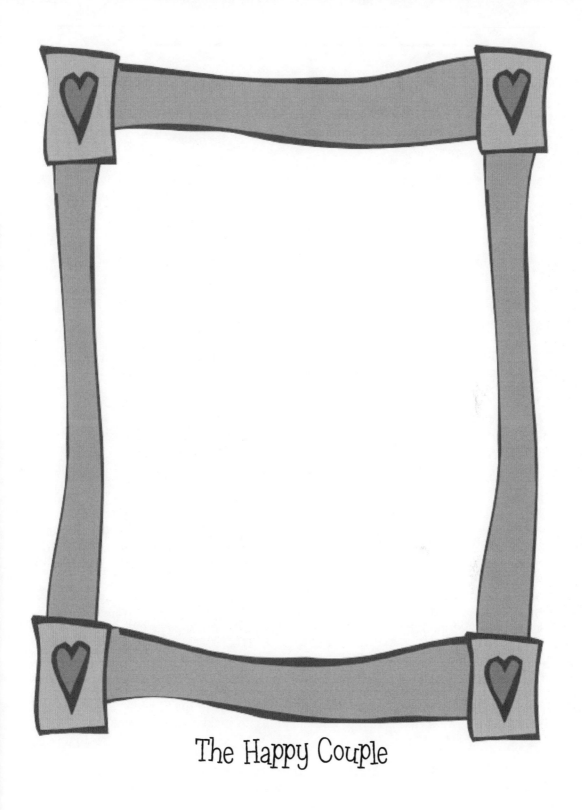

The Happy Couple

Name:_____ Table:_____

Game instructions are on page 71. The answers to the quiz are below. Give them to your game host to score the quizzes and read the extra info, if desired.

1.a In the olden days, dowries were required as an incentive to marry a woman. If the bride was poor or if her father refused to provide a dowry for her (perhaps because her fiancé was a schmuck), a bridal shower would be held to collect money and valuable items for the bride-to-be.

2.b Who knew that quickest way to a person's heart was actually through their ring finger?

3.b A woman's girdle used to have many tight and complicated knots that the groom had to undo before the couple could... you know... canoodle.

4.c Traditionally (and maybe still today!), the bride and groom were considered royalty for a day. Royals were said to have blue blood, hence the "something blue."

5.c Back when indoor plumbing was nothing but a far-off dream, people used to look forward to their annual bath. Flowers masked icky odors coming from any happy couple that didn't manage to wed soon after their bath.

6.b Yup, it's true! And to think that almost everyone in North America chooses a Saturday for their wedding day...

7.c Yeah, it doesn't make sense to me either. People also used to stack cakes as high as possible (leading to the tiered cakes of today) and if the couple could kiss over them without the cakes toppling over, it signified prosperity. Weird!

8.a Hey, it just makes sense: if the evil spirits can't tell the ladies apart, they're less likely to pick on the bride! Another reason is because neighboring tribes used to kidnap brides - identical bridesmaids foiled their evil plans!

9.b Queen Victoria rebelled against the royal tradition of wearing a silver wedding gown in 1840. She certainly set a fashion trend in motion!

10.a I understand the prosperity part, but fertility? In many ceremony locations nowadays, throwing rice is banned because it can make the birds sick, not pregnant.

11.a Octavio Guillen and Adriana Martinez got engaged at just 15 years of age. Sixty-seven years later, in 1969, they finally tied the knot. Now you can't complain that it took you forever to set a date!

12.c You'd want it to rain too if it were 100°F at your wedding!

Wedding Factoids

1. The original purpose of bridal showers was:
    a. to provide a dowry for poor women.
    b. to "cleanse" a bride-to-be in preparation for her wedding night.
    c. to honor the transition to wifehood.

2. Why are wedding bands traditionally worn on the left "ring finger"?
    a. Ancient Romans considered it lucky.
    b. Ancient Egyptians believed your "love vein" ran from there to your heart.
    c. Ancient Mayans believed it to be the location of the soul.

3. The phrase "tie the knot" originates from brides who used to:
    a. be bound at the knees to prevent their escape during the ceremony.
    b. have their girdles tightly knotted to ensure chastity prior to the wedding.
    c. symbolically tie their souls to their husbands for eternity.

4. Why does a bride need "something blue" on her wedding day?
    a. Blue symbolizes honor.
    b. To ward off any "blue feelings" on her wedding day
    c. Blue represents royalty - the bride is queen for a day!

5. Why do brides carry bouquets?
    a. It symbolizes the beauty that the bride brings to her husband's life.
    b. They used to carry fruit, but flowers gradually took over because of famines.
    c. People wanted to mask the smell of stinky brides.

6. According to an old English myth, which is the unluckiest day to get married?
    a. Friday
    b. Saturday
    c. Sunday

7. Wedding cake symbolizes:
    a. sweetness.
    b. prosperity.
    c. fertility.

8. Why did bridesmaids used to dress identically to the bride?
    a. To confuse the evil spirits
    b. To confuse the guests
    c. To confuse the groom

9. Why did brides start wearing white?
    a. It symbolizes purity.
    b. Queen Victoria began the fashion trend.
    c. To save money on costly dyed fabrics

10. People throw rice after a wedding ceremony to:
    a. symbolize fertility and prosperity.
    b. share the couple's good fortune with all of nature.
    c. hide the couple from the devil as they make their escape.

11. The longest engagement on record is:
    a. 67 years in Mexico.
    b. 42 years in France.
    c. 36 years in the U.S.A.

12. In India, it's good luck to have:
    a. sparrows fly over the ceremony.
    b. an even number of wedding guests.
    c. a rainy wedding day.

Game instructions are on page 125. It's best to photocopy pages 191 and 192 double-sided so the quiz is only on one piece of paper. The answers to the quiz are below. Give them to your game host to score the quizzes. To read the original excerpt, do an Internet search for "how to be a good wife 1950."

1.c Yes, husbands of the 1950s were under absolutely no obligation to divulge their whereabouts to their wives. A good wife just kept that yummy dinner warm for however many days/weeks/months it took for her man to reappear.

2.d The old adage "Children should be seen and not heard" definitely applied in the 1950s. No toys, no noise, no purple popsicle mustaches... I guess the idea was for him to be able to forget he had children at all!

3.b "Here, honey, let me undo those tight laces for you. You've had a hard day." If I lived in the 1950s, I'd ask my man to invest in some slip-on loafers!

4.a Again, your 1950s home should be of museum quality - clean and quiet! (I bet some wives sometimes felt (d) was a much better option.)

5.c If you answered (d), all I have to say is, "Hahahahahahahahahahaha!" You wish! Always have a scrumptious, piping hot dinner ready on time for your man. No hot dogs or takeout allowed.

6.b Yup, you're confined to the house, so build that fire, serve that whiskey, and keep your mouth closed. Sounds like marital bliss to me!

7.a Every good 1950s wife knows that your home must be as silent as a tomb in order for your husband to like living there, so vacuum on your own time. (Insert eye-rolling smiley here.)

8.d Although any of these answers *may* be true, the best answer is (d). Don't forget, everything about your hubby is more important than anything about you!

9.a "Exercise his will." Don't you just love that? I just *love* that.

10.b It's straight from the textbook: "A good wife knows her place." Sweet mother of Moses! Try not to hit someone - I know you're mad, but this is a party!

11.c "Oh, honey, you left the kids... where? Cracktown? Okay, I trust your judgment!" Aren't you so glad it's not the '50s anymore?

12.d I'm surprised they didn't just replace wives with robots! I guess they figured they still needed someone to grow the babies...

How to Be a Good Wife

1. How should you react if your husband stays out all night?
a) Freak out, demand details, and make him sleep on the sofa for
a week.
b) Explain how worried you were and that in the future, you'd prefer
a phone call.
c) Just be glad you've got a hubby at all and don't ask questions.
d) Listen to his explanation and then decide how to react.

2. How should your kids greet dad when he returns from work?
a) They should have clean hands and faces.
b) They should be very quiet.
c) They should be asleep.
d) All of the above

**3. What's the best way to make your husband comfortable when
he comes home?**
a) Ask about his day and tell him about yours.
b) Remove his shoes, speak softly, and get him a pillow.
c) Praise him for his success at work.
d) Give him lots of loving hugs and kisses.

4. Right before your husband comes home, you should:
a) dust the house and pick up the kids' toys.
b) put on some sexy underwear.
c) make sure the bar is well stocked.
d) leave the house.

5. What kind of dinner should you prepare for your man?
a) Something gourmet and fancy that includes dessert.
b) Something quick and easy so you don't spend your whole night in
the kitchen.
c) Whatever it is, it had better be delicious and on time.
d) Wait... isn't it his turn to cook?

6. Which is above and beyond a wife's call of duty?
a) Building a fire for your husband to unwind by
b) Getting a part-time job to help pay the bills
c) Never complaining about anything, ever
d) Having his favorite drink ready the moment he walks in the door

7. Vacuuming while your husband is at home:
a) is strictly prohibited - his home should be a haven of peace and quiet.
b) shows him that you care about attending to your wifely duties.
c) should be done by the children so you two can spend time together.
d) signals that you have too much to do during the day and that you need help.

8. You should always let your husband speak before you because:
a) he has more to say than you do.
b) he thinks what you say is boring.
c) then you'll get to have the last word.
d) his topics of conversation are more important than yours.

9. Your husband can always be trusted to:
a) exercise his will fairly and truthfully…. aren't you lucky?
b) be appreciative of your efforts as his wife.
c) admit that he is not really master of the house.
d) bring home the bacon.

10. A wife's biggest no-no is:
a) not participating in making big family decisions.
b) not knowing "her place."
c) not mentioning her concerns.
d) not making her husband's favorite meal.

11. It's always okay to:
a) question your husband's judgment, as long as it's really important.
b) not look perfect when he comes home - you've had a long day!
c) try to please him even if you've had the worst day of your life.
d) complain if he does something really outrageous like crash the car or forget to pick the kids up from summer camp.

12. Which of the following is not part of your goals as a wife?
a) Keeping your hair and makeup pretty for your husband
b) Making the evening entirely your husband's by catering to his every whim
c) Ensuring all areas of the house your husband is likely to see are completely clean and tidy, with no evidence of messy children
d) All of the above are required by a wife of the 1950s.

Bachelorette Scavenger Hunt

Game instructions are on page 145. (White this line out!)

* Have a man serenade the bride.
* Dance with a stripper.
* Get a man's boxer shorts.
* Ask a blond for their phone number.
* Dance on your table!
* Photograph a urinal.
* Kiss a strange man.
* Kiss a strange woman.
* Sip a drink from between a stranger's thighs.
* Buy a drink for the freckliest guy you can find.
* Kiss the first guy to walk into the room with his hat on backwards.
* Get a man to buy someone a drink.
* Get one man to buy each of the bridesmaids a drink.
* Ask a stranger for a condom.
* Have someone sign your bra.
* Buy something icky from an "Adults Only" store.
* Collect the chest hairs of three different men.
* Get a picture with the hairiest man you can find.
* Moon someone from the limo/cab.
* Flash your knockers!
* Get a foot massage from a stranger.
* Give the bartender a pair of undies.
* Kiss a cop.
* Convince the cop to handcuff the bride for a photo op!
* Collect the horoscopes of everyone at the party.
* Start a chat with a stranger by pretending you recognize them from high school.
* Get someone's chewed gum. (Ew!)
* Steal a traffic cone.
* Get a picture of the ladies posing on a hot sports car.
* Get a picture of everyone inside someone's hot sports car!

Oh no, I Never!

Game instructions are on page 148.
Enlarge these cards on your photocopier if you'd like them bigger.
Use the blank cards on page 198 to include your own ideas.

I've never made out
in an elevator.

⁺ABG⁺

I've never stuffed
my bra.

⁺ABG⁺

I've never lied about
my age.

⁺ABG⁺

I've never had sex
in a public place.

⁺ABG⁺

I've never gone
skinny-dipping.

⁺ABG⁺

I've never stolen
anything.

⁺ABG⁺

I've never been in a men's washroom (not counting before you were potty-trained).

+ABC+

I've never sunbathed in the nude.

+ABC+

I've never used a sex toy.

+ABC+

I've never cheated on a boyfriend.

+ABC+

I've never seen a stripper.

+ABC+

I've never used food in the bedroom.

+ABC+

I've never strip-teased for a significant other.

+ABC+

I've never had a one night stand.

+ABC+

I've never worn a skirt without underwear.

ABG

I've never smoked marijuana.

ABG

I've never had liposuction or any kind of cosmetic surgery.

ABG

I've never had sex in a vehicle.

ABG

I've never been tied up during sex.

ABG

I've never had sex on an airplane.

ABG

I've never thrown up in public.

ABG

I've never masturbated in front of another person.

ABG

I've never kissed
another woman.

ABC

I've never kissed two
different guys in
the same night.

ABC

I've never gone out
with a married man.

ABC

I've never had a
homosexual dream.

ABC

I've never faked
an orgasm.

ABC

I've never sneaked out
of the house.

ABC

I've never lied about
my weight.

ABC

I've never been drunk
enough to black out.

ABC

www.TheAlternativeBride.com

Bachelorette Bingo

Game instructions are on page 150.
Enlarge these cards on your photocopier if you'd like them bigger.
Use the blank card on page 202 if you need to make extra cards or
if you'd like to make your own with names and/or different words.

Bachelorette Bingo

mother-in-law	penis	panties	wedding	bachelorette
porno	awesome	honeymoon	foreplay	butt
bridesmaids	boss	come on	stripper	smoking
Kama Sutra	something old	doggy-style	ceremony	take it off
bartender	date	make out	tongue	hot

Bachelorette Bingo

hot	virgin	g-string	sexy	father-in-law
vibrator	playboy	perfume	underwear	boobies
maid of honor	cake	dance	dollar bill	excited
registry	something new	missionary	music	shots
waitress	kiss	worst	hammered	pregnant

Bachelorette Bingo

flower girl	hairy	phone sex	marriage	bachelor
something blue	garter	flight	do it	stripper
kitchen	hungry	limo	mother-in-law	super
erotic	balls	position	gifts	drunk
crazy	socks	fingers	muscles	beautiful

Bachelorette Bingo

sex toy	in-laws	beach	aisle	stomach
presents	whipped cream	music	flirting	dirty
best man	dress	movies	naked	pot
blender	elevator	public	something old	pee
sex on the beach	wine	X-rated	piercing	proposed

Bachelorette Bingo

groomsmen	dye	lingerie	party	single
gifts	cold feet	vacation	attractive	porno
wedding	sex	missionary	dancer	candy
suck	something blue	first date	ring bearer	wasted
game	flirting	makeup	wax	heavy

www.TheAlternativeBride.com

Bachelorette Bingo

ring bearer	cold feet	bikini	engagement	wet
bouquet	69	wedding night	wasted	DJ
shooters	implants	taxi	groom	awesome
cell phone	penis	throw up	cocktail	vibrator
bachelor party	thong	lipstick	bartender	amazing

Bachelorette Bingo

tequila	wax	belly button	diamond	bride
porn star	manicure	Kama Sutra	sexy	honeymoon
vows	attractive	presents	bra	alcohol
garter	foreplay	something new	erection	tongue
bachelorette	our song	chocolate	massage	night

Bachelorette Bingo

make out	fiancé	g-spot	ceremony	boyfriend
drinks	nervous	sex	blow job	jewelry
holiday	martini	shoes	smoky	hilarious
orgasm	date	in-laws	RSVP	loud
whatever	underwear	sweaty	bathroom	cab

Bachelorette Bingo

hair	girlfriend	turned on	doggy-style	marriage
borrowed	alcohol	lingerie	sex toy	flight
porn star	DJ	suck	pick up line	bouquet
balls	girls	drunk	dirty	sleep
engaged	babies	vodka	stranger	shower

Bachelorette Bingo

limo	money	hand job	turned off	kitchen
exotic	position	vomit	one night stand	elevator
bachelor party	orgasm	cell phone	X-rated	weird
interesting	margarita	bridal	skinny dipping	chocolate
flower girl	spicy	hard	bridesmaids	kiss

Bachelorette Bingo

www.TheAlternativeBride.com

Big Night Out

Game instructions are on page 152.
Use the blank cards on page 205 for your own ideas!

Go to a strip club. The first girl to put a dollar in a dancer's g-string chooses the next envelope!

Go bowling. The girl with the most strikes gets to choose the next envelope!

Go to the nearest pub. Everyone must order a drink. Take turns rolling the dice. If you roll anything with a six or adding up to six, you don't have to drink. If you roll snake eyes (two ones), you must do a shot. Any other roll is one big sip of your drink! The person who finishes her drink first gets to open the next envelope.

Go to a bar and put on fake accents. The first person to get asked what country she comes from gets to open the next envelope.

Get manicures. The girl whose nails dry first opens the next envelope.

Go play pool. The girl who sinks the fewest balls gets to open the next envelope!

Go to an X-rated video store. Whoever discovers the most ridiculous movie title gets to choose the next envelope.

Visit an "Adults Only" store. Whoever finds the grossest item opens the next envelope.

Get out the dice. Everyone makes a prediction about how many sixes will be rolled in one minute. Take turns rolling the dice. Whoever's guess is closest without going over opens the next envelope.

Go to a casino and play the slots with five dollars each. The lady who wins the most (or takes the most time to lose) gets to choose the next envelope.

Go to a nightclub and get as many hunky men as possible to dance with the bride-to-be. Let her choose the next envelope!

Find a convenience store. Everyone must buy an item for the bride and explain its significance. The bride chooses who will open the next envelope.

Visit a karaoke bar. The first girl(s) to get up and sing can choose shots for the rest of the ladies to do. The last person to sing gets to open the next envelope.

All ladies must go to the restroom in a nightclub and put on all their underwear over top of their clothing. Start dancing! The first person to get a comment on their apparel opens the next envelope.

Wedding Buzzword

Game instructions are on page 158.

Bouquet *ABG*	The Chapel of Love *ABG*
Pop the question *ABG*	Garter *ABG*
Lingerie *ABG*	Nuptials *ABG*
Buffet dinner *ABG*	Cocktails *ABG*

The Wedding March ABG	Traditions ABG
Pipe organ ABG	Father of the bride ABG
Wedding planner ABG	White Wedding ABG
Centerpieces ABG	Wedding favors ABG
Caterer ABG	Boutonnieres ABG

Something old,
Something new,
Something borrowed,
Something blue. *ABG*

Four Weddings and
a Funeral *ABG*

Here Comes the Bride *ABG*

Wedding gown *ABG*

Ring bearer *ABG*

Flower girl *ABG*

Flower petals *ABG*

For richer,
For poorer *ABG*

Three-tiered cake *ABG*

Rice *ABG*

Scrapbook *ABG*	Honeymoon *ABG*
"His and Hers" towels *ABG*	Engagement *ABG*
Videographer *ABG*	Guest list *ABG*
RSVP *ABG*	Out-of-town guests *ABG*
Outdoor wedding *ABG*	Bridesmaids *ABG*

Bachelor party	Bridal shower
ABG	*ABG*

In-laws	Meet the Parents
ABG	*ABG*

First kiss	Mortgage
ABG	*ABG*

Tuxedo	First dance
ABG	*ABG*

Disc Jockey	Hors d'oeuvres
ABG	*ABG*

Champagne toast *ABG*	Wedding vows *ABG*
Thank-you cards *ABG*	Anniversary party *ABG*
Spa treatments *ABG*	Final fitting *ABG*
Cold feet *ABG*	Wedding registry *ABG*
Groomsmen *ABG*	Wedding night *ABG*

Don't Say It!

Game instructions are on page 160.
Enlarge these cards on your photocopier if you'd like them bigger.
Use the blank cards on page 217 if you'd like to make your own
cards using people's names and/or different words.

Wedding dress

* Bride
* Gown
* Wears
* Clothing

ABC

Bouquet

* Hands
* Bride
* Flowers
* Carries
* Holds

ABC

Garter toss

* Bride
* Leg
* Wears
* Bachelors
* Throws

ABC

I do

* Vows
* Ceremony
* Marry
* Words
* Say

ABC

You may kiss the bride

* Lips
* Married
* Groom
* After

ABC

Father of the bride

* Ceremony
* Parent
* Aisle
* Movie

ABC

Something borrowed

* Old
* New
* Blue
* Bride

In-laws

* Family
* Relatives
* Married
* People
* New

ABC

Will you marry me?

* Proposal
* Engaged
* Question
* Pop

www.TheAlternativeBride.com

Caterer

* Serve
* Food
* Reception
* Meal
* Eat

ABC

First anniversary

* Married
* Celebrate
* Wedding
* Year

ABC

Best man

* Groomsman
* Friend
* Brother
* Stands
* Groom

ABC

Maid of honor

* Bride
* Friend
* Sister
* Stands

ABC

Matron of honor

* Married
* Bride
* Husband
* Friend

ABC

First dance

* Couple
* Bride
* Groom
* Reception
* Music

ABC

DJ

* Plays
* Music
* Dance
* Reception
* Person

ABC

Wedding registry

* Gifts
* Presents
* Give
* Get

ABC

Engagement

* Question
* Proposal
* Before
* Wedding
* Married

ABC

Bridesmaids' dresses

* Gown
* Match
* Bride
* Clothing

ABC

Tuxedo

* Rent
* Groom
* Groomsmen
* Wears
* Clothing

ABC

Limousine

* Drive
* Transportation
* Chauffeur
* Vehicle
* Car

ABC

Four Weddings and a Funeral

* Hugh Grant
* Married
* Movie
* Died

Ring pillow

* Kid
* Bearer
* Bands
* Cushion
* Child

Veil

* Face
* Head
* Bride
* Cover
* Hair

Pipe Organ

* Instrument
* Music
* Church
* Piano
* Ceremony

Here Comes the Bride

* Song
* Music
* Wedding
* Aisle

Ceremony

* Wife
* Husband
* Church
* Married
* Vows

Flower girl

* Child
* Kid
* Ceremony
* Basket
* Petals

Wedding night

* Sex
* Evening
* Make love
* After

Honeymoon

* After
* Vacation
* Holiday
* Fly
* Beach

For richer, for poorer

* Vows
* Sickness
* Promise
* Say

Flowers

* Decoration
* Bouquet
* Lilies
* Plants
* Roses

Father-daughter dance

* Music
* Parent
* Move
* Together

214

Ring bearer

* Pillow
* Bands
* Finger
* Child
* Wear

ABC

Wedding lingerie

* Under
* Clothes
* Dress
* Wear

ABC

Our song

* Music
* Dance
* First
* Bride
* Groom

ABC

Wedding bands

* Rings
* Finger
* Wear
* Married

ABC

Going to the Chapel

* Song
* Music
* Married
* Wedding

ABC

Elope

* Married
* Secret
* Ladder
* Las Vegas
* Don't

ABC

Presents

* Gifts
* Registry
* Give
* Get
* Receive

ABC

Photographer

* Take
* Pictures
* Camera
* Album
* Photos

ABC

Priest

* Church
* Wedding
* Ceremony
* Vows
* Officiant

ABC

Shotgun wedding

* Fast
* Pregnant
* Quick
* Baby

ABC

Wedding planner

* Hire
* Help
* Organize
* Reception

ABC

Guest list

* Family
* Friends
* People
* Relatives
* Attend

ABC

Bouquet toss

* Bride
* Flowers
* Throw
* Single

ABC

Fall in love

* Feel
* Together
* Hearts
* People
* Want

ABC

Always a bridesmaid, never a bride

* Expression
* Wedding
* Saying

ABC

Cold feet

* Jitters
* Nervous
* Before
* Wedding
* Scared

ABC

Runaway Bride

* Julia Roberts
* Cold feet
* Stand up
* Doesn't

ABC

Reception

* Party
* Dinner
* Dance
* Eat
* After

ABC

Bachelorette party

* Bridesmaids
* Women
* Stripper
* Before

ABC

Bachelor party

* Stripper
* Groom
* Get together
* Single

ABC

Tiara

* Bride
* Head
* Hair
* Princess
* Wears

ABC

Engagement ring

* Diamond
* Propose
* Jewelry
* Finger

ABC

Wedding cake

* Tier
* Dessert
* Food
* Eat

ABC

Save the date

* Reminder
* Send
* Guests
* Remember
* Wedding

ABC

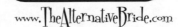
www.TheAlternativeBride.com

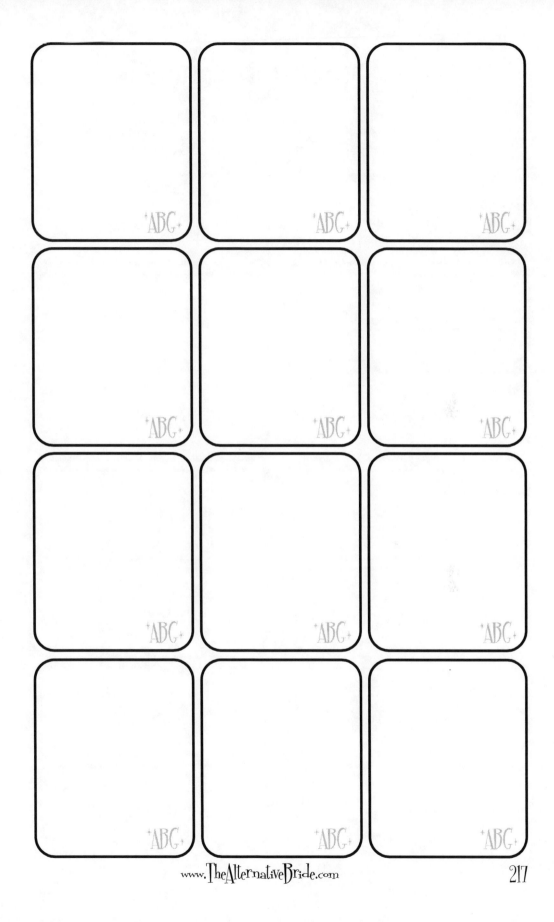

Fast-Paced Foreheads

Game instructions are on page 164.
Enlarge these cards on your photocopier if you'd like them bigger.
Use the blanks on page 221 if you'd like to make additional cards.

Eiffel Tower	Roman Coliseum
Empire State Building	New York City
Toronto	Australia
Statue of Liberty	Mount Everest
South Africa	Paris
The Louvre	Denmark
Switzerland	Great Wall of China

www.TheAlternativeBride.com

Disneyland	Tokyo
North Korea	Canada
Universal Studios	Orlando
The Everglades	Yankee Stadium
Central Park	Cancun
Rio de Janeiro	Brazil
Cuba	Puerto Rico
U.S. Virgin Islands	Leaning Tower of Pisa

Spain	Berlin Wall
Sahara Desert	Rocky Mountains
Alaska	Atlantic Ocean
Dead Sea	Big Ben
London	Wales
Washington D.C.	Great Pyramid
Hawaii	Germany
Antarctica	Stonehenge

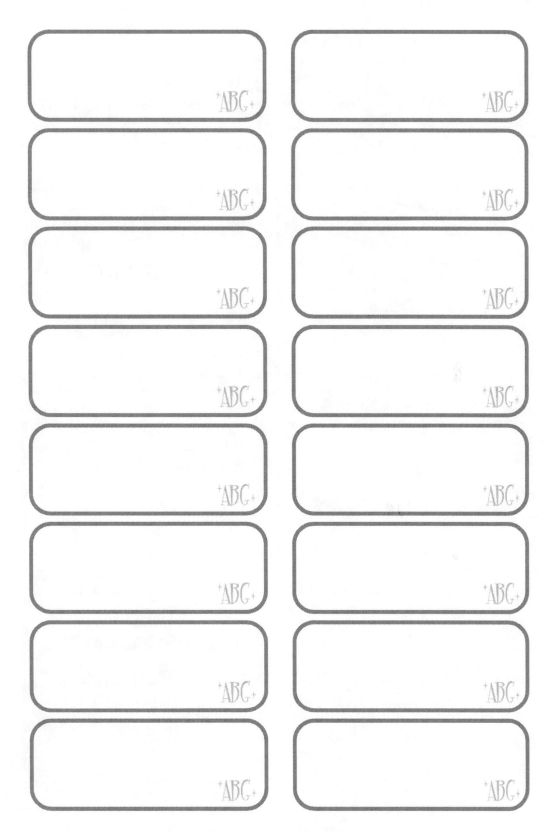

Danger Mime!

Game instructions are on page 167.
Enlarge these cards on your photocopier if you'd like them bigger.
Use the blank cards on page 225 to include your own ideas.

A frying pan is left unattended.

ABG

No burglar alarm is installed.

ABG

The bride and groom never eat their vegetables.

ABG

Too many plugs in the socket!

ABG

No emergency supplies in case of tornado

ABG

The bride and groom forget their sunscreen on their honeymoon to Hawaii!

ABG

A spill is not cleaned up.

ABC

The happy couple sits too close to the TV when watching their favorite shows.

ABC

The newlyweds go grocery shopping on Super Deep Discount Seniors' Day.

ABC

No spare key for the house!

ABC

The groom tells his bride that, yes, that outfit does make her look a little fat.

ABC

The couple forgets to fill up the gas tank before a road trip!

ABC

No one takes the trash out for a month.

ABC

Honeymoon shark attack!

ABC

The cable bill doesn't get paid.

No one salts the icy winter sidewalk!

The couple decides not to make any grandchildren for their parents.

No spare tire!

Nobody checks the expiry date on the milk.

Rollerblades left on the staircase!

Clogged toilet - no plunger!

The bride doesn't wait 30 minutes after eating lunch before she goes swimming!

Visit us on the web at:

www.TheAlternativeBride.com

✳   Browse other ABG titles!
✳   More game ideas!
✳   Share your stories!
✳   Contests and more!

Made in the USA
San Bernardino, CA
30 May 2013